TEN
COMMITMENTS
FOR
MEN

by
Tom Massey

Robert D. Reed Publishers • Bandon, OR

Robert D. Reed Publishers
P.O. Box 1992
Bandon, OR 97411
Phone: 541-347-9882 • Fax: -9883
E-mail: 4bobreed@msn.com
web site: www.rdrpublishers.com

Typesetter: **Barbara Kruger**
Cover Designer: **Grant Prescott**

ISBN 1-931741-59-X

Library of Congress Control Number 2005902194

Manufactured, typeset and printed in the United States of America

*Why do what most men can or will,
when you can do what most men can't or won't?*

Acknowledgments

Thanks to my publisher Bob Reed for challenging me to write a book for men. Your support and friendship have been very meaningful to me throughout the years. Thanks to your staff—Jessica, Grant, and Barbara—for their commitment to excellence and a job well done. And thanks also to Cleone for perusing this book with your keen editing eyes.

Thanks to my business partner and friend Robert Floyd for your help on the book and your willingness to go the extra mile to serve with integrity and the highest degree of professionalism. You personify what this book is about.

A very special thanks to Colin Ingram for your willingness to share your expertise with me and for your candid feedback. You have played a huge part in the future success of this book and the impact it will have on the men who read it.

Thanks to my son Todd and daughter-in-law Dana for your love and never ending support, and to my awesome grandsons Tyler and Paul for reminding me each day of the legacy that will live on through my life. I have no greater joy than to know that my children walk in truth and love.

Thanks to the many teachers in my life who have inspired me to live with passion and purpose. And thanks to the men who read this book and commit these principles to action. You will make a positive difference in our world.

Finally, thanks to God our Father for the great things You have done and will continue to do in all of our lives.

Contents

Foreword

You know the phrase "no new thing under the sun"? Actually, the whole line from the Old Testament Book of Ecclesiastes is "The thing that hath been, it is that which shall be; and that which is done is that which shall be done: and there is no new thing under the sun."

So it's all been done and there's really nothing new? I guess that could be said about books on self-improvement. After all, there are in excess of 100,000 of them currently in print—even Tom Massey, himself, has published several previous books on becoming successful.

Now I know something about these kinds of books, having written, co-authored or edited . . . oh, perhaps 100 of them over the years. And maybe that gives me a kind of credibility when I say that Tom Massey's *Ten Commitments for Men* contains the greatest amount of wisdom I have ever seen in a book of this kind; wisdom that is augmented by some of the liveliest, entertaining and revealing stories you are likely to read.

That pretty much says it all. What can I say beyond this? Well, in his Introduction, Tom suggests a way to read this book. So I will, too. Since this is a book of great wisdom, how should you approach it in order to get the most benefit from it? For one, a degree of neutrality is important; that is, agreeing to be open to ideas on how to live your life . . . at least temporarily, while you are reading. But more than that, there is the concept of reading with an open mind. Now I don't mean merely paying lip service to being open-minded, but really being open-minded.

But what does it feel like to be really open-minded and how do you get there? Here's one way that's helpful. Can you recall ever listening to something very, very attentively—perhaps a subtle passage of music or a softly bubbling brook? Do you remember how it feels to be quietly, fully alert like that?

Pretend for a moment that you are at rest in a deep and silent forest. It is perfectly safe and you are relaxed and comfortable, with nothing to do but admire the beauty and peace around you. Suddenly, you hear an exotic call of a bird you have never heard before. It sounds once, twice and then the forest is completely still again.

What do you do? You become alert to the slightest sound. Your normally busy thoughts stop. Any mood you were in temporarily dissolves. And for this moment your senses are fully alert and your mind is calm.

Now place yourself in that forest right now. Listen closely for the bird to call again and hold this state of listening for several seconds - - - - - - - - - -

This is what it is like to experience a fully open mind. It is a deceptively simple tool, but one that allows your most sensitive and powerful faculties to effortlessly emerge. When you listen, or read, in this state of openness, you will automatically be combining your most acute intellect with your deepest intuition, and your ability to comprehend becomes awesome.

This is a book that encourages and rewards an open mind, and this is how I recommend you approach it.

No new things under the sun? Perhaps, but there are always, always new ways of saying them and new stories to tell. Out of the 100,000-plus books on self-improvement, this book stands out as one of the best. Read it and see.

Colin Ingram

Introduction

A young father was watching a football game on television one Sunday afternoon. His eight-year-old son was in the room trying relentlessly to get his daddy to play with him. The newspaper was spread open on the coffee table with a full-page ad showing a picture of the world as seen from a satellite view from space, and the man got a great idea for keeping his son occupied. He took a pair of scissors and cut the page up into over a dozen pieces, then gave them, along with some cellophane tape, to the young boy saying, "Here, put this picture of the world together with this tape and show Daddy how smart you are." Then he went back to watching his football game.

Within a surprisingly short amount of time, the boy returned with the picture all taped back together in an impressive fashion for a child so young. The father said, "Son, that's really amazing. How did you put that world together so quickly?"

"Daddy, it was easy," the small boy replied. "There was a picture of a man on the other side. So, I just put the man together and then the world came together." The father gave his son a big hug and said, "That's right, son, when the man is together, his world comes together, too."

A monumental moment in life arrives when you discover the truth that things may happen around you, and things may happen to you, but the most important are the things that happen *in* you. When the man is together, his world comes together.

This book will help you put together your life puzzle. Gain practical insights for developing a balanced, purpose-driven life based on what you value most and what you really want. Discover the power of your word to create personal credibility and significance. Explore your passions and develop the courage to take risks. Build quality relationships through making others feel important. Improve your health and learn the value of self-discipline in establishing habits that improve your quality of life. Let go of regrets and become fully engaged in the present to learn and grow to new levels of personal performance. Enhance your productivity and creativity through engaging in fun and laughter. And finally, become a difference-maker who leaves the world a better place.

To assist you in implementing the principles in this book, I have included a series of *Questions and Actions* at the end of each chapter. I suggest that you simply read the book straight through first to become mentally connected to the flow of ideas. Then work back through it slowly, mentally chewing on a new chapter each week, every two weeks, every month, or in whatever time frame you choose. Knowledge is best learned through action.

Chapter 1

Commit to Knowing and Being Yourself

"Destiny is not a matter of chance,
it is a matter of choice."
—William Jennings Bryan

The voice at the end of the telephone said, "Hello, you have reached my answering machine. Actually it is here to ask you two questions: 'Who are you and what do you want?' Leave a message and think about those two questions."

Who are you? Most of us when asked that question respond by describing our societal roles—"I'm a father." "I'm a brother." "I'm a son." "I'm a husband." Or by what we do for a living—"I'm an engineer." "I'm a consultant." "I'm a carpenter." "I'm a salesman." "I'm a musician." But who we are is defined by more than the roles or positions we fill.

When asked that question you might also respond by describing unique gifts, talents or skills that you bring to the world . . . or the type of personality you have . . . or what inspires your soul . . . or what gives you meaning and purpose. Basically, all of these things in some way reflect your self-identity—who you think you are.

Who Do You Think You Are?

"For as a man thinks,
so he is."
—Solomon (Proverbs 23:7)

A frog and scorpion were sitting beside a river one day. The scorpion asked if he could catch a ride on the frog's back across to the other side. The frog said, "Uh, I don't think so." The scorpion asked why and the frog responded, "Because you're a scorpion and scorpions sting frogs. If you sting me I'll die!" The scorpion said, "Don't be ridiculous, mister frog, if I stung you then I would die, too!"

The frog thought about it for a moment and said, "Okay, that makes sense. Hop on." Half way across the river, guess what happens? The scorpion stings the frog! The frog is incredulous. On his third time going down he said, "I can't believe it! You stung me, but now you're going to die, too. Why?" The scorpion shrugged and replied, "Because I'm a scorpion, and that's what scorpions do. They sting frogs!"

This silly old fable characterizes the absurdity of human behavior. Men will do anything they can to make their actions congruent with what they think or believe about themselves, regardless of how destructive or tragic it may turn out to be. If you want to permanently change your life, you must change your thoughts and beliefs about who you are.

The first step in living at your highest potential is to develop a positive self-identity. How you see yourself and how you feel about yourself will have a tremendous impact on what you will accomplish in life. *You will never rise above the image you have of yourself in your own mind.* What you believe is what you will achieve.

How can you change the image you have of yourself? Begin by using your self-talk in a positive, life-changing way. The words *I am* are the two most powerful words in your vocabulary. These words personify the very essence of creation. In fact, they personify the essence of the Creator. You may recall the story of Moses (Remember that Old Testament prophet who looked a lot like

Charlton Heston?) in his encounter with the burning bush on Mount Horeb. Moses received the command to go on a heroic journey and he posed the question, "When I tell them the God of their fathers sent me, and they say to me, 'What is his name?' What shall I tell them?" The Voice from the flames responded, "Tell them *I AM* sent you!"

When you use the words *I am* in a sentence you, too, become a creator. Every cell in your body perks up, cups their ears, and listens just like in an E.F. Hutton commercial. You literally begin to affect positive changes from the inside out when you use positive affirming statements such as "I am a man of valor" or "I am a man of integrity" or "I am a man of excellence!" And if you repeat these statements often and long enough, your sub-conscious, that powerful sleeping giant within your mind, will awaken and respond to ensure that they become true in the world of form.

How you see and describe your life is important. If I asked you how you view your life, what would that image look like? That image is called your life *metaphor*. This is your life story held either consciously or unconsciously in your mind. For instance, if you see your life as a battle, then winning will be very important to you. If you see life as a party, your primary focus will be having fun. I saw a bumper sticker once that said, "Life's a bitch and then you die." Imagine what life is like for the man who professes that. According to an ancient proverb, our words fall over us and wrap themselves around us like a cloak. I wouldn't want those words wrapped around me, would you? Be careful with the metaphors you use for your life because the words you attach to your experience *become* your experience.

Your expectations, your relationships, and your goals are all affected by your life metaphor. How do you describe your life? Are you basing your reality on a faulty, negative metaphor? If so, it's time to starting repeating a different story. If you want the circumstances in your life to improve, you must think it and you must speak it.

Who Do Others Say You Are?

"Your playing small doesn't
serve the world."
—Nelson Mandela

My father was raised in a very poor farm family during the Great Depression era of the late 1920s and early 1930s. He quit school in the eighth grade to work in the cotton fields to help his family. He was an honest, hard-working, and good man, but because of his upbringing, my father had a poverty mentality and poor self-image throughout his life.

I remember when I first decided to go to college, he questioned why. "Son, I have always been a poor working man—my father was a poor working man and so was his father," he said. He went on to convey his belief that I was also destined to be the same and that going to college wasn't "for the likes of people like us." From his perspective the best thing for me was to get a job and live my life in the quiet resignation of being a poor laborer.

That was one of the earliest and most powerful motivational speeches I received in my life. I was fiercely determined to break out of that mold. Consequently I earned four college degrees to prove that success *is* for "people like us." Don't misunderstand what I'm saying here—there is no disgrace in being poor or being a laborer. But it is tragic to let other people or circumstances influence your estimation of your worth.

You may have encountered tough experiences in your life. Perhaps you were rejected or told that you would never amount to anything. You may have been the kid that always sat on the bench or the last one chosen when sides were split up for a ball game. Regardless of the situation you are still valuable. Imagine that I just handed you a crisp, new one-hundred-dollar bill. Would you want it? Probably so! What if I crumpled it up in my hand so it wasn't as good-looking as it was when it was new and crisp? Would you still want it? Most certainly! And what if I took it out to the street, threw it down and stomped on it until it was oil stained and dirty? Would you still want it? Of course.

A hundred dollars is still a hundred dollars regardless of whether it is new and crisp, or tattered and soiled because that's what our government has declared it to be worth. You are like that hundred-dollar bill. Regardless of your ancestry, past challenges, struggles, or failures, you are a man of value. *Stand up and walk in the light of who you are!*

What Do You Want?

"Most people aim at nothing in life,
and hit it with amazing accuracy."
—Dale Carnegie

A cartoon appeared in a local newspaper that depicted two men, manacled in chains, rowing in the galley of a slave ship. One said to the other, "I always wanted to be somebody, but I should have been more *specific*."

The act of naming and claiming what you want is one of the most important principles of success that govern our world. Not knowing precisely what you want is not acceptable. If you cannot name, and name with great specificity, what it is that you want, then you will never be able to step up and claim it.

That great philosopher Yogi Berra once said, "If you don't know where you're going, you might end up some place else." Unless you are very specific about what you want in life, you may end up with a lot of things you *don't* want. That's an all too familiar situation for many. From past experience, you may speak with great confidence about the things you don't want. Therein lies a danger, because of the universal law of attraction, the more you focus on what you don't want, the more of it you will get. And *you can never get enough of what you don't want!*

Men who live lives of significance are very deliberate about the pursuit of their life goals. They know specifically what they want, then fix their sights and take aim with careful precision. Ready-aim-fire—decisiveness creates action, and action leads to results.

Don't be shy about the fact that you want extraordinary things in life. You deserve them! Acknowledge and honor the special feelings of self-worth, significance, and fulfillment you gain from receiving those things. Be ambitious, yet realistic with your goals. Aim for a realistic target that you can hit, but don't set your sights too low and spend your life working for things you don't want. What you want is yours for the asking, but be specific.

Ask yourself the following questions:

- What do I really want in life?
- Why do I want it?
- What am I willing to do to get it?
- Who do I need to enlist to help me get it?
- How will I feel when I get it?

Repeat the process with a partner. Be honest, be sincere, and be specific. The more you practice this, the more you will produce what you really want in your life. Write some positive affirming statements directed toward each of those five areas, repeat them often, and expect great things to happen.

Don't be afraid to ask others to help you get what you want. Men of vision and power have one characteristic in common: They know how to ask for what they want. For them, asking with passion is a natural way to make continuous progress on the path to success. Asking is a catalyst for change. Martin Luther King, Jr., changed the course of our country's history because he asked people to share his dream of equality for all people. Mahatma Gandhi changed the course of his nation by asking his fellow countrymen to join him in peaceful revolution to win autonomy for India. Winston Churchill rallied his country against a Nazi invasion by asking his countrymen to, "Never give up!"

Each day presents opportunities to ask for what you want. Pay attention to those moments and boldly step forward to make your requests known. And don't ever assume that people know what you want or need. It is your responsibility to make this known—*if you have not, perhaps it is because you have asked not.*

By asking today for what you want, you will plant the seeds that will enable you to enjoy tomorrow's harvest of success and prosperity. And let go of the belief that asking reveals weaknesses or glitches in your armor. We all need assistance from others at times. There is no shame in asking. If it was good enough for King, Gandhi, and Churchill, it's good enough for you. Ask with laser-like clarity and be specific. Ask with confidence and boldness. Ask with persistency and don't fold up your tent after one timid request.

Become a Man of Value

> *"Try not to become a man of success,*
> *but rather try to become a man of value."*
> —Albert Einstein

Jim is a talented guy . . . creative, articulate, clean-cut, nice-looking, and well-liked. He is the kind of person that opportunities seem to swoon over. At times this becomes a problem for him because he easily becomes sidetracked.

I tried to persuade him to identify his core values and some specific goals so he would have a sense of clarity over what is really important in his life. One day he came into my office very excited. He had been offered a new position with a national company and was contemplating taking it. I was a little surprised because it seemed to be a complete 180-degree turn from the direction he had been going. After discussing it, he admitted that the job didn't really interest him all that much and the company was not one he particularly wanted to work for. I asked why he would even consider it. He admitted that it was so flattering that they would seek him out for the position that he was reluctant to turn down the opportunity.

Growing a little exasperated, I said, "Darn it, Jim, you don't have to crawl into bed with everyone who blows you a kiss!" He said, "Excuse me?" I responded, "You are a talented guy and no doubt many opportunities will come your way. Some will be right for you, but many will not. Why don't you clarify what's really important, so when opportunities do arise you will have a better idea of deciding which is which."

How about you? Do you sway in the wind like a reed or are you firm and solid like a rock? When you clarify what is most important, you will be more centered and have a better sense of direction about where you're headed.

I share my own core values, along with actions, below to give you an example of how to define and use these. When you define your values, it is helpful to describe the actions or behaviors that reflect those in your life. If you don't put them into action, are they really a core value?

<u>**Values**</u>	<u>**Actions**</u>
Relationships	Spend quality time with God, family, close friends and business associates to validate, appreciate, encourage, and support on a daily basis.
Health	Exercise regularly, maintain a healthy diet and lifestyle, manage weight, manage stress, and choose a positive and cheerful attitude.
Integrity	Keep my word, speak the truth in love, and practice personal accountability without excuses.
Excellence	Sharpen my saw daily through reading, continually improve language and vocabulary skills, perform ongoing research for new material in presentations, and solicit constant feedback to provide outstanding service for clients with no excuses.
Simplicity	Stay single-minded and focused on what I do best, keep my workspace and personal life organized without clutter, and stay debt-free.

Whenever opportunities arise I always check my list of values and ask the following questions: Can I do this without neglecting my most important relationships? Will this jeopardize my health in some way? Can I maintain integrity in this? Do I have the ability or time to perform this with excellence? Can I do this and maintain simplicity without weaving tangled webs for myself? If the answer to any of these questions is "no," I must seriously assess whether this is a wise choice for me.

Find Your "One Thing"

"This is the true joy of life: the being used up for a purpose recognized by yourself as a mighty one."
—George Bernard Shaw

You may recall the movie *City Slickers*, starring Billy Crystal and Jack Palance. Crystal played the part of a tenderfoot from Los Angeles who paid for a two-week dude ranch vacation to inject a spark back into his life. His wife insisted that he take the trip and told him to go "find his smile" again. Palance played a wily cowpoke named Curly who was tough as nails. There is one particular scene in the movie where they are riding across the range on horseback, discussing life and love. Listen to their slightly edited conversation:

Crystal: *"You ever been in love?*

Palance: *"Once, when I was driving a herd across the panhandle of Texas. Passed by this little dirt farm right about sundown. Out in the field was this young gal working down in the dirt. Just about then, she stood up and stretched her back. She was wearing a little cotton dress, and the settin' sun was right behind her showin' the shape that God gave her."*

Crystal: *"What happened?"*

Palance: *"I just turned around and rode away."*

Crystal: *"Why?"*

Palance: *"I figured it wasn't going to get any better than that."*

Crystal: *"Yeah, but, but you could have been, you know, with her."*

Palance: *"I've been with lots of women."*

Crystal: *"Yeah, but she could have been the love of your life."*

Palance: *"She is."*

Crystal: *"That's great. No . . . that's not great, Curly. You passed up something that could have been terrific."*

Palance: *"My choice."*

Crystal: *"I could never have done that."*

Palance: *"That's your choice. But cowboys lead a different kind of life."*

Crystal: *"You see, now, that's great. Your life makes sense to you."*

Palance: (Chuckles)

Crystal: *"What? What's so funny?"*

Palance: *"You city folks. You worry about a lot of s---, don't you?"*

Crystal: *"S---? My wife just told me that basically she doesn't want me around."*

Palance: *"She a redhead? I like redheads."*

Crystal: *"I'm just saying . . ."*

Palance: *"How old are you? Thirty-eight?"*

Crystal: *"Thirty-nine."*

Palance: *"Yeah. All you guys come out here about the same age. Same problems. Spend fifty weeks a year getting knots in your rope, then you think two weeks up here will untie them for you. None of you get it. (Long pause) Do you know what the secret of life is?"*

Crystal: *"No, what?"*

Palance: *"This."* (He holds up his index finger)

Crystal: *"Your finger?"*

Palance: *"One thing. Just one thing. You stick to that and everything else don't mean s---."*

Crystal: *"That's great, but what's the one thing?"*

Palance: *"That's up to you to figure out."*

Many men never discover their "one thing." And what is so unsettling is that they know it's there somewhere. Like Billy Crystal's character, we all desperately yearn to find it. It's like a hollow place located in the core of our soul.

To live a life of significance and fulfillment, you must find your one thing . . . that purpose for which your life stands for. It might change or evolve over time, but you have to start somewhere. You may find your one thing "out there" someplace or you may find it within you. Regardless of where, find it. Ask . . . listen . . . observe . . . experiment . . . take some risks. Stay curious and live in the question. Whatever it takes, seek until you find that one thing that is so compelling that you can't let it go.

Hold on to Your Vision

> *"If one advances confidently*
> *in the direction of his dreams*
> *and endeavors to live the life*
> *which he has imagined,*
> *he will meet with a success*
> *unexpected in common hours.*
> *He will pass an invisible boundary;*
> *new, universal, and more liberal laws*
> *will begin to establish themselves around*
> *and within him; and he will live the license*
> *of a higher order of beings."*
> —Henry David Thoreau

A number of years ago a group of journalists was given a tour of the EPCOT Center at Disney World in Orlando, Florida. Their guide explained that Walt Disney had a dream in the early 1960s of building an entire city. This city would be called the *Experimental Prototype Community of Tomorrow*, or EPCOT for short. It would be a model community that would serve as both an example for optimal living and a laboratory to test solutions to problems that other cities face, such as urban unrest, suburban sprawl, increasing crime, air and water pollution, overtaxed roads, and over taxed citizens.

Disney bought thousands of acres of land in Florida and convinced the Florida Legislature to grant his company the power to drain, dredge, and develop the land into his dream city. He threw himself into this "Florida Project," which was to consume his final days. First he planned to build a theme park and resort, which would be used to pay for the rest of the development. Although he had already built Disneyland in California, the world's most successful theme park, the EPCOT Center proved to be his greatest challenge.

Walt Disney died in 1966, his plans far from complete. Roy Disney, Walt's brother, continued to carry on with his work. Magic Kingdom Theme Park and its associated hotels that comprised Walt Disney World opened in October 1971. The EPCOT dream fell by the wayside at that time, but was reborn again a decade later. EPCOT Center opened on October 1, 1982, over twenty years after Walt Disney had conceived his dream.

After the tour guide told this story to the visiting journalists, one young writer gazed up at EPCOT Center and quipped, "It's too bad the old man didn't live to see it!" The guide quickly retorted, "Oh, Mr. Disney saw it all right. If he hadn't, it wouldn't be here today!"

Visionary men have a knack for "seeing the unseen." Viktor Frankl, the renowned Viennese psychiatrist who survived years of torture in a Nazi concentration camp, once spoke these words to an audience: "There's one reason why I'm here today. What kept me alive in a situation where others had given up hope and died was the dream that someday I'd be here telling you how I survived the concentration camps. I've never been here before. I've never seen any of you before. I've never given this speech before. But in my dreams I've stood before you in this room and said these words a thousand times."

Life becomes what you envision it to be. *If you see it, then you can be it*. You will never rise above the image you have in your mind because you will continually produce on the outside what is in the inside. If you think little, believe little, and expect little, then you will receive little.

One of the most common slogans among men who are serving long sentences in prison is, "You've got nothin' comin'." They have no income, their children are embarrassed to say they are related to them, their wives don't come see them, and nothing is going to change in their lives. They don't expect anything better or think they deserve it. They've got nothing coming.

Sadly, many men "on the outside" are living in self-imposed prisons of their own making. What they're getting is the best they can expect. They think that life is not going to get any better, so they may as well sit down, shut up, and accept it. If you're in that prison, break free. The door isn't even locked! Begin by expecting good things to happen in your life. If you want your life to change for the better, you must first see it change in your mind. You must imagine yourself as happy, successful, and that you have "great things coming!" *To achieve great things you must conceive great things.*

When you become clear about whom you are and what you want, your life will take on an exciting newness. You will bounce out of bed in the morning with a spring in your step. Your work will be gratifying and even the most mundane tasks will take on new meaning.

Questions and Actions

1. Who are you and what do you want? What's working in your life and what isn't? Be honest as you reflect on your current life circumstances. Don't make excuses and don't lay blame. Simply make adjustments in your life based on what you've learned. If you are willing to acknowledge a circumstance, and take ownership of your role in it, you can create the positive change you desire for your life.

2. Choose your language carefully and stay positive. Create personal statements that you will use repeatedly to affirm who you are in a positive light. Repeat those statements throughout the day to yourself and out loud if possible. Make them your daily mantra. The more often you repeat them, the more effective they will be. Be personal, be positive, and use action words that arouse passion.

    For example:

    *   I am successful!
    *   I am a man of courage!
    *   I am a difference-maker!
    *   I am healthy and vibrant!
    *   I am a man of integrity!

3. Decide what you want and set some S.M.A.R.T. goals to help you get it:

- **S**pecific—Name exactly the expected outcome.
- **M**easurable—Determine how you will evaluate and measure your progress.
- **A**ttainable—Be realistic, yet stretch yourself.
- **R**elevant—Each goal should be congruent with your core values.
- **T**ime Driven—Define a specific date for completion or milestones to be measured along the way to your goal accomplishment.

4. What gives depth and meaning to your life? Identify what is most important to you. Choose four or five core values for which you stand and list key actions which confirm that these are your values. In other words, others should be able to observe your life and know these are your values by your actions. Who you are speaks louder than what you say!

5. Do you have a vision for your life? What would your life look like if it were perfect? Use the creative power of your mind to *clarify* and *specify* what you want to achieve in life. Set aside some time each day to capture a mental picture of what you desire. Close your eyes and imagine your life to be successful and meaningful. Mentally touch it, smell it, and feel it down into the depths of your being. The more vividly you create your vision at the mental and emotional levels, the more powerfully it will be materialized into the physical world. Finally, cast aside all doubt. You *will* see what you believe!

Chapter 2

Commit to Being a Promise-Keeper

> *"Your word is the most powerful tool*
> *you have as a human."*
> —don Miguel Ruiz

Your words are powerful. So powerful in fact that one word can positively change a life or destroy it. In the book, *The Four Agreements*, don Miguel Ruiz reveals a powerful code of conduct that can transform one's life into a new experience of personal freedom and happiness. The first of the four agreements, which Ruiz says is the cornerstone of personal transformation, is to *be impeccable with your word*.

Impeccability with your word will cause you to be at peace with yourself and others as you instill a sense of trust in all relationships. It will especially help you to develop a heightened sense of self-worth. Alexander Pope said, "An honest man is the noblest work of God."

Men of significance establish personal credibility through keeping their word. When they make promises, they make every effort to keep them. If you want to experience success and significance in your life, whether in your relationships or in your career, it is imperative that you keep your word.

Own Your Actions

"It is our responsibilities, not ourselves,
that we should take seriously."
—Peter Ustinov

A certain King, who lived centuries ago, fell in love with a beautiful young woman. However, there was one glaring problem with this relationship; the woman was married. Not only was she married, her husband was a loyal officer in the King's army. The plot thickened when the woman turned up pregnant with the King's child, and in his desperation to have her for himself, the King finagled a plan to place her husband on the front lines of battle to face sure death.

The King's oldest and wisest advisor got wind of the whole sordid affair and confronted the King with a story about a rich man with many flocks and a poor man who had nothing but one little ewe lamb, which he had bought, nurtured, and loved. One day the rich man stole the little ewe lamb from the poor man and had it served up in a feast for one of his houseguests. This story incensed the King who angrily declared, "The man who has done this deserves to die, because he had no pity!"

The old advisor sternly responded, "Sire, you are that man!" The guilt-ridden King gazed sadly into the old sage's eyes and replied, "I, and I alone, have committed this wrong."

You may recognize the King, his name was David—a man of large proportions both materialistically and spiritually. He was reputedly the wealthiest man in the world at that time. And the scriptures later referred to him as "a man after God's own heart"— largely because of his humility and willingness to be accountable for his actions. The King could have rebuffed the old prophet Nathan and had his head removed, but instead chose to humbly acknowledge and assume personal responsibility for his actions. He still faced some looming consequences for his past actions, but David didn't make the mistake of weaving more tangled webs for the future by making excuses for himself or passing the blame.

When you have lapses of judgment or make mistakes, own up to them without excuses. Taking responsibility for your actions is one of the most important keys for establishing personal credibility.

Be a Man of Character

"Our character is what we do when
we think no one is looking."
—H. Jackson Browne

A young man and woman were headed to a nearby lake to spend some quiet moments alone. They decided that a picnic would be nice, so they stopped to pick up some fried chicken on the way out of town. The man went in and ordered a box of chicken, while the woman waited in the car. The person who took his order boxed up the chicken and set it down on the counter beside an identical box that contained the money and receipts from the previous workday, which the manager intended to take to the bank for deposit. After the man paid his bill, the person at the counter mistakenly handed him the box of money instead of the box that contained the chicken.

On their way to the lake, the couple opened the box and discovered the mistake. The man immediately turned the car around and headed back to the restaurant to return the box of money. The manager of the store greeted him with elation. He told the man how relieved he was that the money had been returned, as he went on and on about the man's honesty. The manager said he had a friend who was a reporter for the local newspaper and that he wanted to ask his friend to write a news story lauding the man's good deed.

The man thanked the manager for the offer but refused to give him his name. He told him that he did not want him to go to the trouble of reporting the story. The manager kept insisting, refusing to take "no" for an answer. Finally the man sheepishly replied, "Sir, you can't report this to the newspaper. You see, I am a married man and the woman I am with is not my wife!"

The man in the story demonstrated that honesty and integrity don't always ride on the same bus. Men of character live and walk with integrity, even when no one is looking. They are completely trustworthy because their lives are built upon a solid foundation of impeccability.

Are you walking in integrity? Do you think you are the only one who knows when you are not? Regardless of what measures you take to conceal secrets in your life, your actions will ultimately reveal those secrets to the world. *Someone is always watching.* And reproof often comes in the most unsuspecting moments.

Without integrity you will never reach your highest potential. As Will Rogers once said, "Live your life in such a way that you wouldn't be afraid to sell the family parrot to the town gossip."

Your character should be based on who you are, not what the situation is. I once counseled with a couple who had been facing difficulties in their marriage. The man was old school—always performing kindly gestures like opening the car door for his wife. During the course of their marriage she became unfaithful to him. He was really hurt by her actions, but he continued to open the car door for her. She began to feel guilty about it and asked him, "Why do you continue to open the door for me after all I've done to you?"

"I don't open the door for you because of what you do or don't do," he replied; "I open the door for you because of who I am— *I am a gentleman.*"

Don't Look Where You Don't Want to Go!

> *"What you look at the longest*
> *becomes the strongest thing in your life."*
> —Mike Murdock

A few years ago when I first learned the skill of rappelling, I was gazing with apprehension off the hundred-foot cliff from which we were getting ready to rappel to the valley below. With frantic thoughts of plummeting to the ground I moaned, "That's a looong way down there." My guide sensed my fear and replied, "Don't look where you don't want to go." What a great philosophy for life!

What you think about expands in your life. If you think positive thoughts, you attract positive things into your life. The same goes for negative thoughts. You might ask, "What does this have to do with being a promise-keeper?" Often when you make a promise or commitment to do something, the temptation arises to renege and do something else. Stop trying to "resist" temptation because *what you resist will persist.* Instead, focus your attention on what you want.

Each time you try to block a thought out of your mind, you simply drive it deeper into your memory. So by resisting a thought, you actually reinforce it. And what holds your attention will arouse your emotions, which in turn activates behavior. Ignoring a temptation is a far more effective strategy than simply trying to resist it. Once your mind focuses on something else, the temptation loses its power. For example, say you made a commitment to quit an unhealthy habit. The next time that you have the urge to give in to the habit, don't try to resist the desire; simply redirect your mental focus to something else. If you will do that for a mere thirty seconds, the urge will diminish drastically. *When temptation calls, don't argue with it. Simply hang up the phone!*

Let me caution you: If you keep breaking promises to yourself and you're losing the battle to a persistent unhealthy habit or some other temptation that has you stuck in a repeated cycle of *good intentions—failure—guilt*, the likelihood of you getting better on your own is slim. You need the help of others. You don't have to broadcast your struggles to the whole world, but you do need to seek out at least one other person with whom you can trust and be totally honest. Some temptations can only be overcome with the help of a partner or support group who will encourage you and help hold you accountable.

You will know you are a candidate for outside help if there is something in your life you're pretending isn't a problem or you're too embarrassed to talk about it. You're simply not going to solve these types of problems on your own. I know (too well!) that it is humbling to admit your weaknesses to others, and most men have a particularly difficult time doing that. But a lack of humility is the very thing that will block you from getting better and growing through this.

Make Excellence a Habit

> *"We are what repeatedly we do. Excellence, then,*
> *is not an act, but a habit."*
> —Aristotle

What does it mean to be a man of excellence? It means making the effort to do what's right. It means keeping your word when it's difficult. It means arriving at work on time every day and giving your employer a full day's work. When you possess an attitude of excellence, it shows up in the quality of everything you do.

Begin to practice excellence each day in your personal life. For instance, practice good personal hygiene—keep your hair combed, brush your teeth regularly, and trim your nose hairs. And make sure that you wear fresh, clean clothes each day. You may not be able to wear the most expensive clothes, but they can be clean. Your personal appearance is a reflection of how you feel about yourself. If you leave the house looking sloppy and wearing dirty clothing, you're not going to feel good about yourself.

Keep your car washed and clean on the inside. When you drive a car that hasn't been washed in two months with a backseat filled with junk, it doesn't represent a man of excellence. You might be driving an old clunker, but you can still keep it clean and take pride in what you have. And if you do so, you will begin to feel better about yourself and attract greater things into your life.

Take care of your home. Keep your lawn mowed and your house clean and uncluttered. You might not live in a big, new home, but at least you can keep it looking nice. You may live in an area where the entire neighborhood is messy, but don't let that rub off on you. Be the one who stands out in the crowd—a man of excellence!

Show respect for and take good care of others' property as if it were your own. If you are leaving a hotel room, don't leave the lights on, the T.V. blaring, or the air-conditioner going full blast. It doesn't matter if you are paying for the room. You wouldn't waste electricity at your home, so don't waste it at someone else's.

These are subtle actions that will help you to be and do your best. Make a habit of going the extra mile even when nobody is watching and don't settle for mediocrity. Live your life devoted to excellence, and you will be happier and will attract excellent things into your life.

Questions and Actions

1. What do people say about your word? Is it impeccable? Are you a promise-keeper? Honesty must start with you. Are you honest with yourself? When you truly commit to keeping your word,

you will begin to see exciting new changes happening in your life. First you will see changes in the way you deal with yourself. How you feel about yourself is directly proportionate to the integrity of your word. Second, you will experience changes in your relationships as they become more open. Third, you will reap tremendous gains in success and abundance in your work by developing a reputation of impeccability. This does not mean that you can do or be all things to all people. Learn that it is okay to say "No." In fact, it is much better to give an honest "No" than to say "Yes" and not keep your word.

2. Do you have an accountability partner? Many great men have fallen because they became disconnected from a source of accountability. Choose one or two close friends with whom you can confidentially share an alliance of trust and feedback. I know that men are notorious for not sharing personal information; but if you want to learn and grow, you must be willing to be engaged in honest relationships with other men who are willing to be real.

3. What has your attention? Are you looking to the sky with anticipation or the ground with dread? *Don't look where you don't want to go.* The things you are "for" will strengthen you while the things you are "against" will weaken you. Stay positive. Keep your mind focused on what you want instead of what you don't want.

4. Are you committed to excellence? Perhaps you have made some mistakes in the past, but don't let that hold you back. Do the honorable thing and make it as right as you can. And don't just do what you have to do to get by. Go the extra mile. Pay those past debts back with interest and keep your relationship accounts cleared. View others as an extension of yourself and treat them as you would want to be treated.

Chapter 3

Commit to Getting Excited about Something

"Most men die with their music still in them."
—Oliver Wendell Holmes

The story is told of a dispassionate young man who approached the ancient Greek philosopher Socrates and nonchalantly stated, "Oh, great Teacher, I come to you for knowledge." Socrates took the young man down to the sea, waded in with him, and then dunked him under the water for thirty seconds. When he let the young man up for air, Socrates asked him to repeat what he wanted.

"Knowledge, oh great One," he sputtered. Socrates put him under the water again, for a little longer, and repeated the question. The response was the same. After repeated dunkings, each a little longer with similar responses, Socrates held him under for a particularly long time, then asked again, "What do you want?" The young man gasped, "Air! I want air!"

"Good," answered Socrates, "Now, when you want knowledge as much as you wanted air, you shall have it."

What do you want as much as air? What keeps you awake at night because of your passion? Don't be one of those men Oliver Wendell Holmes described as dying with their music still in them. Sociologist Tony Campolo recently observed: *"We are caught up at a particular state in our national ethos in which we're not only materialistic but worse than that; we're becoming emotionally dead as people. We don't sing, we don't dance, we don't even commit sin with much enthusiasm."*

Your enthusiasm will ultimately influence your success more than your personality or intelligence. If you want something badly enough you will get it. *The world will make way for the man who knows what he wants and pursues it with passion.*

Be a Risk-Taker—Go For It!

> *"For of all sad words of tongues or pen*
> *the saddest are these: It might have been."*
> —John Greenleaf Whittier

Bob Manley, a copy editor for a Cleveland newspaper, was a man some people might have called eccentric, or even downright crazy. Dreaming of retracing the immigration route of his ancestors, he set his sights on sailing from Falmouth, Massachusetts, to Falmouth, England.

For less than a few hundred dollars, Bob purchased a thirty-year-old sailboat that measured only thirteen and a half feet. He refurbished the boat and practiced sailing on Lake Eerie for several months. To avoid hearing the discouraging words of naysayers, he shared his plans only with his wife.

On the day of embarkation, Bob kissed his wife goodbye and set sail on the 3,200-mile voyage, tying himself to his boat, in case he encountered rough seas that threatened to toss him overboard. This turned out to be a wise precaution, because he was thrown from the sailboat, several times, by storm-tossed waves. To make matters worse, he had to remain awake at night to avoid entering the shipping lanes. With his sleep limited to daytime naps, Bob became delirious and exhausted. Yet he sailed onward.

Seventy-eight days later, he sailed into the harbor at Falmouth, England, to a reception of over twenty thousand people who had heard about his remarkable feat. Because of his outstanding achievement, one U.S. congressman submitted a bill to place Bob's boat, "Tinker Bell," next to Charles Lindbergh's "Spirit of Saint Louis" in the Smithsonian Institute. When asked why he would attempt such an incredible challenge, Bob Manley simply answered,

> *"There comes a time when one must decide*
> *either to risk everything to fulfill one's dream,*
> *or sit for the rest of one's life in the backyard."*

In the heart of every man is the desperate desire to experience an adventure in life. But that adventure has a cost. Men of significance are risk takers who are willing to act upon their vision and dreams. They are undaunted by the pessimistic "we've never done it that way before" crowd. They set their course and weather each storm in pursuit of this daring adventure called life. These men are much less concerned with fitting in than standing out.

Men throughout history who have left their footprints in the sands of destiny were driven by a passion greater than their desire for personal comfort. You can possess great potential and even know that you have a significant purpose in your life, yet fail to move beyond good intentions to experience the fullness of life—unless you are willing to move beyond your comfort zone. Do you allow your personal comfort to be an obstacle to success? *You won't change anything that you are willing to tolerate.*

What are you tolerating in your life that keeps limiting you? Begin to take small risks that will enable you to stretch in incremental units or steps. The more you stretch, the greater capacity you will have to grow.

Write Yourself a Hot Check

> *"The individual activity of one man with backbone*
> *will do more than a thousand men with a mere wishbone."*
> —William Boetcker

A friend shared about a time when he was a young man serving in a local civic organization. He had volunteered to be the leader for a major fundraising project established to benefit city firefighters. The project involved selling booklets compiled of discount coupons from local merchants for food, theater tickets, auto repair, cleaning, and various other professional services. The organization advertised that customers could purchase the book for about twenty dollars and save hundreds in discounts from the merchants. The profit from the sale of each book was to be donated to purchase new firefighting equipment.

He recounted how someone in the organization ordered a large quantity of the coupon books and specified that they be delivered to his house. What they didn't tell him was the order would be shipped C.O.D. (cash on delivery). He said he was relaxing at home one Saturday morning when the books arrived. He looked at the sum on the invoice in a state of shock, knowing that he didn't have the funds in the bank to cover what seemed like a large amount of money at the time.

I asked him what he did and he said, "At that point I didn't have many options, so I did what any normal, red-blooded American would have done. I wrote a check for it—a hot check!" He went on to explain that he called five men who had previously volunteered to help him with the project. He emphatically explained that they needed to get busy and sell these books—today! He said that he refused to take "No" for an answer and that his compelling sense of urgency became contagious as each man agreed to take immediate action. They recruited others to help and enough books were sold over the weekend to cover his check as he hurried to the bank the first thing Monday morning to make a deposit.

The endeavor was such a success that he went on to win a state award that year for leading the top fundraising project in the organization. That same tenacity has propelled him to the top of his profession today as he regularly shares this message: *"If you really want to succeed, write yourself a hot check to create a sense of urgency. Anything you want enthusiastically enough will be yours."*

I am not saying to literally begin writing hot checks for what you want. Your bank or your creditors won't appreciate that. But I do believe that it is a good thing to write yourself a hot check figuratively, in your mind, so that your mission becomes so compelling that there is absolutely no way to retreat. A friend told me that he once asked a successful musician how to start a band. The guy's response was, "Book a gig. That will motivate you to get started!" Even Thomas Edison would reputedly make a public announcement about an invention he had not yet completed, then retreat to the lab to make it happen.

If there is something that you have been aspiring to do, write yourself a hot check and set out to accomplish the task. Book a gig. If you want to get started with something pick a date on the calendar and commit to it. Create a sense of urgency that will drive you toward success.

Decide—Then Act

> *"It is in your moments of decision*
> *that your destiny is shaped."*
> —Anthony Robbins

Lester Wunderman wanted to work in advertising. He found a job with an advertising firm in New York and worked as an apprentice studying under Max Sackheim, one of the great minds in the field at that time. Things didn't work out the way he planned and Lester was fired from his job. Motivated by the decision to learn what Sackheim could teach him, he continued to show up at his office every day—without pay. After a month of this, Sackheim walked up to him and said, "Okay, okay, you win. I never saw a man who wanted a job more than he wanted money. You can have your job back."

Lester Wunderman went on to become one of the most successful people in advertising in this century. So successful, in fact, that many refer to him today as the father of direct marketing. And it all began with a decision followed by action.

The word "decision" comes from the Latin roots *de*, which means "from," and *caedere*, which means "to cut." Making a true decision means committing to an action, then cutting away every other possibility. If you truly decide to stop drinking alcohol, you no longer consider the possibility of being a drinker. If you truly decide to stop smoking, you no longer consider the possibility of being a smoker. If you truly decide to be healthy, you no longer consider the possibility of practicing unhealthy habits.

Think about a time in your life when you made a true decision. You may have struggled or sat on the fence for some time before you committed to take action, but remember how it felt once you finally did. Did you feel relieved? Even energized? It is in these moments that you really shape your destiny.

Here are three important questions that will influence your future:

1. What do you value most in life?
2. What do you want?
3. What are you willing to give for number two to happen?

First, decide what is most important. Next decide what you want, making sure it is congruent with your values. Then count the cost. What are you willing to "cut away" to get what you want?

In his book *Awaken the Giant Within* Anthony Robbins describes a phenomenon that he calls the "Niagara Syndrome." He compares life to a river where most people jump in without ever deciding where they want to end up. They float aimlessly down the river and get caught up in the various currents—*current events, current fears, and current challenges.* Whenever they encounter forks in the river, they simply "go with the flow" rather than make a conscious decision about which way to go. They become like the masses of others who are directed by circumstances rather than their own values. They often feel out of control. Sound familiar? They remain in this unconscious state until one day the sounds of raging waters awaken them, and they discover that they are five feet from Niagara Falls in a boat with no oars. At this point, they shout, "Oh, shoot!" or some other choice words, as they take a fall—which may be emotional, physical, or financial. The message is:

Whatever challenges you are currently facing
in the river of your life
may well have been avoided
by some better decisions upstream.

Are You Committed or Merely Involved?

"If you make the unconditional commitment
to reach your most important goals,
you will find the way
and the power to achieve them."
—Robert Conklin

In 1519 the Spanish conquistador Hernando Cortez led an expedition to Mexico with 400 men. One night, with the soldiers safely ashore, he burned all their ships so that turning back became impossible. This left nowhere to go but forward. Although outnumbered they won victory after victory, and his military triumphs led to 300 years of Spanish dominion over Mexico.

Although you may not lead a military conquest, you will certainly face formidable foes that require you to "burn the ships" to ensure total commitment in order to move forward without retreat. *There's no such thing as a 90% commitment—you're either committed or you're not.* Consider the analogy of eating ham and eggs for breakfast. The pig was committed to your breakfast, while the chicken was only involved. How about you? Are you committed to something exciting and worthwhile in life, or merely involved?

Questions and Actions

1. What is your passion, the spark that only needs a gentle wind to ignite into a raging fire in your soul? Think back to when you were just starting your career, or even farther back to when you were a child. What really got you jazzed? Go back and recapture that old enthusiasm. If you've lost that "fire in the belly," find some people who have it and hang out with them for a while. Enthusiasm is contagious. Let it rub off on you. And make it your burning desire to become the most passionate man you know.

2. Find work you love to do. When you do what you love to do, no one has to motivate you or challenge you. Think about the

three things in life that you like to do the most (sex and eating don't count). Somewhere in this list lies a vocation that you can become passionate about. Seek out people who are doing work you want to do and ask them for advice on how to get started.

3. Are you a risk-taker? Do you push yourself to the limits? *Why not go out on a limb? That's where the fruit is!* You have the power to do things you never dreamed possible. This power becomes available to you as soon as you are willing to step beyond your fears. You know what you are today, but not what you may become tomorrow. Look at life as you want it to be, and then make things happen. Bold intentions lead to courageous actions, which result in astounding outcomes. Go for it!

4. Are you ready to make a firm commitment to something? If not, what is standing in the way, and what will it take for you to make that commitment? Begin today by taking a step in the right direction. Find a cause or something in which you can become fully committed. *We all come into life with a one-way ticket, so don't worry about saving anything for the return trip.*

Chapter 4

Commit to Building Quality Relationships

"No man is an island unto himself,
each is a part of the main."
—John Dunne

Not one person in history ever succeeded alone. We are each part of the main continent of humanity. Each of us is designed by our Creator to be incomplete—everyone needs someone. As we grow, we move from a state of dependence as small children, to one of independence as men, but it is not the final stage. Beyond independence is the stage of interdependence, where we understand and accept that we cannot accomplish anything significantly on our own.

I don't care if you are one of the most self-contained, rugged individualists in the world, you need people. Face it! Even the Lone Ranger needed Tonto. We all need companionship—someone who takes our part when the problems of the world seem to take us apart.

Connecting with others and building relationships are the greatest sources of pleasure *and* pain, in our lives. Love is a two-sided coin, as you well know. Building relationships is a risky business because the pendulum of love swings two ways. You must be willing to risk the pain to experience the pleasure. If you stop the pendulum you won't experience either, therefore it is better to have loved and lost, than to have never loved at all.

Acknowledge Others

"Men will die for ribbons."
—Napoleon Bonaparte

Many years ago, when my son Todd was a child, we regularly took walks together in the woods. Being a typical rambunctious young boy, he never walked beside me. Rather, he would constantly run ahead, then stop and wait for me to catch up. One day while on one of our walks, he ran ahead of me, then crawled up on a big rock and sat down to rest. When I caught up with him, he said, "Daddy, let's just sit on this rock and talk for a while." I climbed up on the rock beside him and said, "Okay. What do you want to talk about?" He responded with utmost seriousness, "I don't care, just as long as it's *important!*"

And so it is with each of us. We all have an innate need to feel important to those around us. Everyone wants to count for something—to be acknowledged and respected. When you make others feel as though who they are and what they have to say is important, they will give every ounce of strength to show their loyalty back to you.

Acknowledging others may cost little in terms of tangible items, such as money. But it will cost one of your most priceless resources: *time*. Your time and attention are the most valuable gifts you will give to others.

Reach Out and Touch Someone

"I make holy whatever I touch
or am touch'd from."
—Walt Whitman

The deepest desire in the human experience is to be touched. In *The Russian Revolution*, Richard Pipes tells how deeply this need runs in humanity: "During the atrocities that accompanied the

Boshevik revolution in Russia, thousands of bewildered suspects were randomly arrested, rounded up, stripped naked, and shot one by one in the back of the head. One eyewitness account captures the depth as well as the poignancy of our need to feel linked, joined together: 'Most of the victims usually requested a chance to say good-bye; and because there was no one else, they embraced and kissed their executioners.' "

Touch is our most essential, yet most neglected sense. We can survive without sight, without hearing, without the sense of taste, or smell. But we cannot survive and live with any degree of comfort or emotional health without touch. Studies have shown that children who are not touched as babies have a much higher incidence of violence and dysfunction in their adult lives. The absence of human touch produces life that is purposeless and chaotic, and in acute cases causes psychotic breakdown or even death.

A study in an orphanage during wartime showed that many babies who were not touched or talked to at all, except what was absolutely necessary in feeding and clothing them, *literally died—* whereas the ones who were touched and given attention *lived!*

Touching comes in many forms. You don't necessarily have to physically contact someone to touch them. You can touch others with the look in your eyes, or the tone of your voice, or sometimes simply with your presence. Author and lecturer, Leo Buscaglia, once described a contest he was asked to judge. The purpose of the contest was to find the most caring child. The winner was a four-year-old boy whose next-door neighbor was an elderly gentleman who had recently lost his wife. Upon seeing the man sitting on his porch crying, the boy went into the old gentleman's yard, climbed onto his lap, and just sat there. When his mother later asked what he had said to the neighbor, the boy replied, "Nothing, Momma. I just helped him cry."

A group of graduate students were given an interesting assignment by one of their professors. She gave each of them three buttons with the words "Who You Are Makes a Difference" on them, then proceeded to tell them how special they are and how they had made a difference in her life. The professor then told them to "pay it forward" by seeking out and presenting one of the buttons to a person who had made a difference in their life and to express their own appreciation. The students were instructed to give a second button to this same person and ask him or her to pass it on to someone in his or her life.

One young man in the class decided to give a button to the man who ran the company he worked for, expressing to him what a positive influence the man had been in his life. The owner of the company was quite touched and a little surprised by the gesture. The young man told his boss about the school project, then gave him another button and asked him to pass it on to someone that "made a difference" in his life.

The man thought some time about who might be the recipient of his button and decided to give it to his sixteen-year-old son. When the man got home from work that evening, he went to his son's room and slipped the button into his hand. He hugged the boy and told him what a difference he had made in his life and how proud he was to be his father.

Upon listening to his father's words, the son began to weep. He confessed to his father that he felt like a failure. In his despondency the boy had decided take his own life that very night and put an end to his anguish. He even had the suicide note already written. But fortunately, this father's well-timed words served as a lifeline to rescue a young son drowning in hopelessness and despair.

Have you ever been discouraged and had someone come along and lift you up with a few words of encouragement? A little can go a long ways, especially to someone who is dangling at the end of his rope. You never know when you might cast someone a lifeline of hope just through the power of touching them with your words.

Mend Your Fences

> *"Forgiveness does not change the past,*
> *but it does enlarge the future."*
> —Paul Boese

Many years ago I worked as a caretaker on a cattle ranch. One morning I was awakened by a telephone call, and the voice on the other end of the line asked, "Have you looked outside? Your cattle are loose." I rushed outside to see almost a hundred head of cattle, meandering down the road.

I ran to the barn, grabbed a bucket of feed, and took off in pursuit of the herd. A bull was in the lead and I stuck the bucket of feed up to his nose enticing him to turn around. As we ambled back down the road with his nose in the bucket, each cow we met turned and followed in single file. I felt like the Pied Piper of cattle.

After securing the herd, I found a small break in the fence and quickly mended it to prevent future escapes. The break seemed tiny compared to the size of a cow. It surprised me that such large beasts were able to slip through, as I shuddered to think of the havoc that might have been caused if they had made it to the interstate highway less than a half-mile away.

I have pondered that moment throughout the years, as other fences have required mending in my life. Small, seemingly harmless rifts in personal relationships can cause beastly chaos to ensue. Perhaps there are some fences that need mending in your life. Is there someone with whom you have had a longstanding disagreement or misunderstanding? Are you avoiding them or holding a grudge? Holding a grudge against someone else is like swallowing poison and expecting the other person to die.

It doesn't matter who started the rift; it is in your best interest to mend it if possible. Let go of the debate over "who is right?" and "who is wrong?" Make a phone call or send a card or an e-mail to that person and offer an olive branch of peace. The issue is not about whether the other person deserves it or not. Your personal health and well-being depend on it.

When it comes to mending fences and developing quality relationships, there are times that we must let go of our own self-righteousness. Booker T. Washington was the foremost black educator of the late 19th and early 20th centuries. Born a slave on a small farm in the Virginia backcountry, he rose to prominence in 1881 when he founded the Tuskegee Institute in the Black Belt of Alabama. The story is told about an incident that happened to Dr. Washington on his way to his office at Tuskegee one wintry morning. As he walked past a large estate, the woman who owned the place emerged out of the house and, mistaking him for one of the hired servants, shouted orders for him to chop some firewood and bring it inside.

Rather than becoming indignant, Dr. Washington took off his coat and began to chop wood. When he finished, he carried the wood into the house and stacked it, then continued on his way to work. One of the women who worked in the kitchen recognized him and told the owner who he was. The owner was quite embarrassed by her presumptuousness and hastily went to seek him out at Tuskegee to offer her apologies.

When she found Dr. Washington at his office, she apologized profusely and let him know how embarrassed she was about the whole incident. He responded, "That's no problem, ma'am. I love to work and I love to help my friends." The woman, who was quite wealthy, was so touched by his gracious spirit that she reportedly became one of the most ardent and generous financial contributors to Dr. Washington and the Tuskegee Institute throughout the rest of her life. One act of kindness can turn an adversary into a loyal friend.

Refuse to get caught up in the negative. Let go of your need to be right. Your understanding and kindness will be reflected back to you. As you help, you are helped. As you uplift, you are uplifted. Relationships are the fertile soil from which your advancement and achievement in life will grow. *You cannot hold a torch to light another's path without brightening your own.*

Partner for Peak Performance

"None of us is as smart as all of us."
—Napoleon Hill

A book about men of significance would be incomplete without some mention of Bill Gates, who is considered to be one of the most successful men alive today. Although Gates has his faults, he has achieved success on many levels—personal wealth of over $100 billion, a $21 billion charitable foundation, the pervasive influence of his company's products in the market place, and a thriving family life.

Why Bill Gates? What does he have that the rest of us don't have? He's smart but not any smarter than many college graduates today. He is hardworking and determined, but so are millions of others. He is not any more impressive personally than others. In fact, he appears to be shy and a little aloof at times, and often slips into a peculiar hunched rocking motion when speaking in public. What's up with this guy?

What is Gates' secret to success? He is a genius at *finding the right partner at the right time*. If you review his career, you'll find that he has been a serial partner-finder—beginning with his closest childhood friend Kent Evans. Like Gates, Evans was fascinated with computers, but he was more imaginative, persistent, and less inhibited. He pushed Gates to take more risks and think big.

No one knows how successful this partnership might have become because Kent Evans was killed in a climbing accident in May of 1972. His life left a profound impression on Gates who donated a science and math center to his high school in Evans' name. And after over thirty years, Gates says he still remembers his friend's phone number.

Following Evan's death, Gates forged a partnership with Paul Allen, who shared his intense interest in computers. They formed their Microsoft consultancy in 1975 while holed up in a small apartment in Albuquerque, New Mexico, and brought in Monte Davidoff to write a complicated piece of code for their software, but he turned down an offer to become Microsoft's third employee. I suspect that he has had second thoughts about that decision throughout the years.

Next, Gates sought out and hired Steve Ballmer who has been his alter ego for the past twenty-five years. Ballmer is as hardworking and mentally agile as Gates, but more extroverted, louder, emotional and openly passionate. He was the logical choice to become Microsoft's CEO in January 2000 when Gates decided to return to his true love of strategic software design.

You might challenge this deduction by saying, "Hey, he's Bill Gates, of course he can find right partners." But the truth is, he is "Bill Gates" because he possessed the genius for finding the right partners. Look around and you will observe how frequently success and partnership are seen in one another's company.

Regardless of what your dream is, partnering with others will benefit you. It will create an opportunity to help others achieve their goals, as you draw upon their diverse experiences, knowledge, and contacts to help you achieve your own. Don't underestimate who and what you know. Look for ways to help others and build a reputation as being a "giver." You will derive tremendous personal satisfaction from giving and you will advance your own cause as well.

The world faced a tremendous challenge rebounding from the Great Depression in the 1930s. The man at the helm of the ship of recovery for America was Franklin D. Roosevelt who wisely surrounded himself with the advice, counsel, and collaboration of a group of people who were willing to serve in a spirit of unity.

Roosevelt engaged the help of one man, in particular, who was instrumental in organizing the group to help lead the country back to prosperity. Napoleon Hill, author of the book *Think and Grow Rich*, agreed to help the President facilitate the recovery from the Great Depression through masterminding a plan for success.

Hill defined a mastermind group as the "coordination of knowledge and effort, in a spirit of harmony between two or more people, for the attainment of a definite purpose." He believed that "two heads are better than one," and beyond that, the utilization of a team of people could yield an exponential growth in mental capacity. This form of collaborative partnership has been the basis of nearly every great success.

On Love and Marriage

"In the absence of love,
there is nothing worth fighting for."
—Elijah Wood

Robert Fulghum the author of *All I Really Need to Know I Learned in Kindergarten* wrote about a conversation with Alexander Papaderos, renowned Greek philosopher and the director of the Orthodox Academy of Crete. They were discussing the subject of love and marriage. The Cretans think romance is nice enough when it happens, but they don't think it is a particularly good basis for marriage. Papaderos was a little confused over the concept of "making love," which he had read about in Western literature. "What is this making love?" he asked.

Fulghum tried to explain that it was a popular euphemism for having sex—making whoopee, getting it on, going to bed, etc.—whether married or not. Papaderos replied that "making love" is a very serious notion to the Cretans as he summarized the process of marriage and family. In their tradition, when two families agree that a son and a daughter would suit one another, it is expected that over time the man and woman will work at becoming compatible partners in the same spirit that one might work at achieving competence in his life's vocation. This is making love.

Time and experience, along with mistakes and difficulties, are all part of the equation for a lasting relationship. Love is not something two people fall into. Love and marriage are "made" with great deliberation. Thus, when a married couple is overheard arguing or fighting, the Cretans smile and say, "Ah, they are making love."

Love may be blind, but a strong relationship should not be. In a strong relationship, love blindness should be replaced with a practical understanding of who your partner really is. If you cling to an unrealistic version of her, eventually she will fail to live up to it; and that fragile relationship, built on an illusion, will crack and break.

Listen to your partner. Understand that she may see the world differently than you do. Make a clear-eyed assessment of her strengths, weaknesses, and values, which over time will replace the initial rush of romance. Love her for her strengths, while accepting and offering support in her areas of weakness. *Together a perfect whole will be molded from your two imperfect halves.*

Be realistic, yet at the same time look for the best in your partner. According to studies from the Gallup organization, in the happiest couples, husbands consistently rate their wives more positively on every quality than the women actually rate themselves. In other words, the husband who perceives that his wife possesses strengths even she doesn't think she possesses will have a strong marriage today and an even stronger one tomorrow.

Learn to Like Yourself

*"You can't give away
that which you don't have."*
—Unknown

Regardless of where you have been, what you have done, or how you look, you must learn to like and accept yourself in order to experience a personal state of well-being. This doesn't mean that you intend to stay as you are or that you don't have room for improvements in your life. In fact, you're working on getting better every day in every way. Right?

A Hasidic master named Rabbi Zusya once pondered this issue: "If they ask me in the next world, 'Why were you not Moses?' I will know the answer. But if they ask me, 'Why were you not Zusya' I will have nothing to say." Your greatest responsibility is to be who you are and not one thing more. No other man offers the world what you have to offer. *You were born to be you.*

Stand in front of the mirror every day, smile and look yourself in the eye, down into the very depths of your soul, and say, "I like you, man!" Transforming any relationships begins with the simple step of transforming yourself. If you don't learn to care for yourself, you will never really care for others—you can't give away that which you don't have!

Questions and Actions

1. How are you doing at acknowledging the people around you? One of the best ways to make others feel important is to really listen to them. Actively and intently engage others by making eye contact and giving full attention to what they say. Instead of quietly formulating what you are going to say next, simply suspend those thoughts and intently listen to them.

2. Who are you pouring your life into? It won't do much good to conquer the world and ignore your family in the process. Do you treat the pizza delivery guy better than your own kids? Invest your time in the people who matter most in your life and

show them that you really care. If you don't have a positive impact on those closest to you, you are missing the mark.

3. Is there some fence mending that needs to take place in your life? Is there someone that you have been avoiding because of a longstanding disagreement or misunderstanding? If you don't make an effort to do some fence mending, there is a risk that others may get hurt, too. Even the smallest break can wreak havoc in your life and the lives of others. Grab your tools and go mend your fence. Perhaps one of the most effective fence-mending tools you possess is an apology: "I am sorry." It is difficult for another person to fight with you when you are willing to negotiate a truce.

4. Who are you partnering with for success? Learn to build on your own unique strengths and talents, and rely on others with complimentary strengths and talents to make the work you are doing complete. Look for individuals with a blend of skills and experience who are willing to collaborate. Set some meeting times and agreements on how you will mutually benefit from partnering with one another.

Chapter 5

Commit to Taking Care of Your Health

"If you were arrested for being good to yourself,
would there be enough evidence to convict you?"
—Peter McWilliams

As previously mentioned, I was once the caretaker of a ranch. Jack Hall, the old fellow who owned the place, treated me like a son. I was an avid long-distance runner in those days, and each morning I would log between five and ten miles up and down the road that ran in front of the ranch. I really enjoyed those mornings of running the road as the sun came up, smelling the aroma of fresh cow manure on wet grass. I know, you probably think the cow manure thing is strange, but don't knock it until you try it.

Practically every morning, Mr. Hall would sit and watch me run from his office, atop a hill overlooking the entire spread. At the time he was suffering from emphysema and lung cancer, so exercise to him was limited to an occasional walk around the barn.

One warm summer morning as I finished my run, Mr. Hall motioned for me to swing by his office. I stood there soaking wet from an exhilarating workout, feeling euphoric as runners often do. He looked at me wistfully and his words are still etched in my mind. "Son, I'd trade everything I own for your youth and vigor," he said.

The saddest irony of life lies in the fact that "we don't miss the water until the well runs dry." Mr. Hall died less than a year later, but his words live on in my mind. Here was a man of vast wealth who would have willingly traded it all, just to feel good once again. But unfortunately, when it comes to health, we don't often miss it until it's irretrievably gone.

Do not take your health for granted. Goals and dreams matter little when you are sick. For what should it profit you to gain the whole world, and lose your health? Actually, being healthy will enhance your goals and dreams. Physical fitness can lead to fiscal fitness in a variety of ways. First, you will experience less down time because of sickness and poor stress recovery. You will also experience increases in energy and stamina, which will help you to work harder, with greater longevity. Brain functioning, along with self-confidence, is also improved which leads to working smarter and more creatively.

Rejuvenate with Sleep

"Sleep is a reconciling,
a rest that peace begets."
—William Shakespeare

Sleep is the number one recovery factor for stress management. You need an average of six to eight hours per night to adequately give your body time to perform necessary metabolic functions and allow for normal stress recovery. The two most important stages of sleep are called Delta and Rapid Eye Movement (R.E.M.). Both are essential. During the deep Delta stage, sleep produces a growth hormone that repairs body damage inflicted by "free radicals," which are by-products of normal cellular function, exposure to pollutants, and direct or second-hand smoke. Oxygen atoms, which normally have four electrons, under certain conditions can loose an electron and thereby become unstable and reactive. This unstable state is known as a "free radical." If left unchecked, these cells cause heart damage, cancer, cataracts, and a weak immune system. Free radicals are also associated with the aging process itself. As a person ages, cell damage accumulates. Getting adequate amounts of sleep and supplementing the diet with extra vitamins, such as Vitamin A, C, and E, also known as antioxidants, can help slow the oxidative damage done to cells.

Factors that can affect the sleep cycle include:

- Anxiety
- Room temperature
- Altitude
- Diet
- Balance of saturated fats
- Alcohol and other drugs
- Overall stress levels
- Noise outside the room
- Amount of light in the room
- Size and timing of meals
- Ratio of carbohydrates and proteins
- Rapid weight loss

Listed below are some tips that may help you sleep and relieve symptoms of insomnia.

1. Develop regular sleep rituals and follow them.

2. Go to bed and get up at the same time as often as possible.

3. Regardless of when you go to sleep, get up at the same time.

4. Exercise daily but not too close to going to bed.

5. Eliminate long naps during the day if they affect your nightly sleep pattern.

6. Limit caffeine or alcohol intake.

7. Keep your bedroom at a cool temperature, well ventilated, and as dark as possible.

8. If necessary, use relaxation breathing or meditation to quiet the mind.

9. Don't get angry or frustrated when you can't fall asleep. Simply relax and enjoy the quiet time, or grab a book or something (healthy) that will help you relax.

You Are What You Eat

> *"Let food be your medicine;*
> *and medicine be your food."*
> —Hippocrates, 400 B.C.

The setting was city hall in San Francisco. A disgruntled young man named Dan White walked into the courthouse and in a fit of rage gunned down Mayor George Moscone and city councilman Harvey Milk. White's lawyers skillfully crafted a successful defense of insanity, claiming that their client, under duress, fell into an uncontrollable rage brought about, to a great extent, by a diet of junk food. The media later referred to it as the infamous "Twinkie Defense."

As Hippocrates said, food and medicine should be one and the same. Do you find that you are often moody, irritable, and short with people? Has anyone ever asked, "What's eating you?" Maybe the more accurate question should be, "What have you been eating?" Food should naturally boost your performance and enhance your life, not weaken it. A diet high in fruits, vegetables, and whole grains helps your body maintain a balance of health and well-being.

According to the National Cancer Institute, less than 25 percent of all Americans actually eat the foods they should. Instead, most people live on a diet of fast foods that are designed to provide their palates with a carnival atmosphere of taste. As a result, cancer and heart disease have risen at alarming rates. During the 1980s, researchers began to question why cancer and heart disease rates in the U.S. were high compared to other less advantaged countries, in spite of our more advanced medical technology and wealth. Subsequent studies revealed that people who live in those less advantaged countries have diets that are rich in fruits, vegetables, and whole grains, which appear to give them greater protection against cancer and heart disease.

For years, nutritional experts in the U.S. have advocated those "third world diets," that are high in whole grains, fresh fruits, and fresh vegetables. Whole grains contain much-needed nutrients and fibers, as do fruits, which are called the "cleansers" of the body, and vegetables, which are called the "rejuvenators." These fresh, or so-called "live," foods contain digestive enzymes, which enhance cellular reproduction, improve digestion, and boost the immune system. Enzymes, and other nutrients found in fruits and vegetables, help keep the body free of disease and infection.

You may recall the Biblical story of Daniel, who became famous for sitting unscathed in a lion's den. He was a young Jewish man who was transplanted from his homeland and raised in captivity in ancient Babylonia. He was assigned to live in the king's palace and eat the rich food and drink the wine from the king's table. Daniel resolved not to partake in the food from the king's table, and he asked the chief of the palace guard for permission to abstain from eating it. The chief told Daniel that he feared if the king saw Daniel becoming undernourished and looking worse than the others, the king would have the chief's head. Daniel asked his superior to test him and three of his friends for ten days, giving them only vegetables to eat and water to drink. The chief consented. At the end of ten days, he was so impressed with the health and physical appearance of Daniel and his friends, that he ordered all the other men to be placed on a diet of vegetables and water. *A diet high in natural foods will not only fortify your health, it will also improve your appearance.*

You will also increase your mental performance by feeding your brain with a healthy diet. The brain is a relatively small organ compared to the rest of the body, but it is a hungry one. It consumes approximately twenty-five percent of the total energy taken into the body and is more sensitive to nutritional deficiencies than most of the other organs. If you deprive your brain of the right nutrients, even for a short period of time, you may experience problems concentrating, short-term memory loss, or moodiness. Over the long run, a lack of proper nutrition may increase the risk of more serious disorders.

The following nutrients are crucial in manufacturing brain chemicals that enhance concentration, memory, mood, and performance:

- **Amino acids**—These are essential for the proper production and function of neurotransmitters in the brain and may strongly affect mood. They are found in high-protein foods such as meat, poultry, fish, dairy products, eggs, beans, and nuts.

- **Antioxidants**—The brain is more susceptible to free-radical damage because is has a high concentration of fatty tissue. Antioxidants block free radicals, protect DNA, and keep brain blood vessels open and flexible. These are found in berries and dark-red fruits, oranges, dark-red and deep-green vegetables, nuts and seeds, liver, and eggs.

- **B vitamins**—This vitamin family, especially folic acid, B1, B6, and B12, is essential in maintaining brain cells, metabolizing carbohydrates (the brain's food source) and producing neurotransmitters that are important to brain functioning. They may be found in dark-green, leafy vegetables, cauliflower, cabbage, citrus fruits, beans, peanuts, seeds, whole grains, meat, fish, liver, dairy products, and egg yolks.

- **Fats**—Omega-3 fatty acids keep the cellular walls in the brain pliable for receiving and transmitting neural signals. They are found in salmon, herring, mackerel, sardines, tuna, flaxseeds, walnuts, canola oil, and eggs.

- **Iron**—This carries oxygen in the blood to the brain cells and is used to produce neurotransmitters. It is found in dark-green and leafy vegetables, such as spinach, beets, dried apricots, whole grains, and red meat.

One more item worth mentioning in the area of nutrition is *water*. It is essential in the processes of cellular respiration and rejuvenation, energy production, digestion, and detoxification. Your skin, along with every organ in your body, needs it for health and vitality. A good rule of thumb for calculating how much water you should drink is to divide your weight by two—and that is how many ounces you should drink minimally each day.

Get Physical and Exercise

"We're all artist and sculptors;
flesh, blood, and bones
are our materials with which to work."
—Henry David Thoreau

A few years out of high school I became the epitome of the out-of-shape "couch potato." I had grown up participating in sports but settled into a sedentary life after graduation. My lifestyle and eating habits were unhealthy, to say the least. I watched my waistline balloon from 28 to 42 inches in the span of about three years.

An awakening came one night when I went ran into a young woman who had been an acquaintance in high school. I asked if she would like to go to a movie sometime and she consented, but I'm not really sure why. While on our date, she laughed at me and made cruel comments about my weight. She poked her finger into the spare tire around my waist and taunted me by calling me "Chubby." When I attempted to give her a goodnight kiss at the door, she turned her head.

The humiliation cut deeply, but it turned out to be a tremendous motivator. When I arrived home that night, I looked at myself in the mirror and swore that no one would make fun of me again because I was fat. I started doing push-ups and setups each night before going bed. I started running daily, which resulted in a loss of 75 pounds and 12 inches from my waistline over the next six months. I began a weight training regimen and eventually gained 30 pounds of muscle back, while adding only a couple of inches to my waist.

Everyone who dumps on us is not our enemy. This young woman actually performed a great favor for me. Her honesty, which seemed a little brutal at the time, was a wake-up call for me. And it was better to experience the humiliation of her rejection than to experience serious health problems later because of an unhealthy lifestyle and obesity.

Incidentally, I ran into her a few years later in a grocery store. She appeared to have gained most of the weight I lost. No, I didn't rub it in. Instead I humbly thanked her for having such a positive impact on my life.

The human body reciprocates magnificently to how it is treated. If/when you quit smoking, your body will heal most or all of the damage to the lungs. When you stick with a healthy regimen, your body rewards you with more vibrant health and reduced risk of disease. When you roll off the couch, turn off the television, and lace up your walking shoes, your body will thank you with greater energy, stronger bones, and a generous measure of youthfulness. And it's never too late to start. Regardless of how old you are, consistent physical activity will make you feel better physically, mentally, and emotionally.

Scientific research concludes that people of all ages benefit almost immediately from exercise. One study was set up to investigate the effects of a strength and flexibility program on frail, elderly residents in a long-term care facility. After only six weeks of working out three times a week with a combination of weight training and aerobics exercise, participants were able to move around more easily, with significant improvements in balance, physical performance, and mental function.

Moderate weight training is important, especially in older adults, because of loss of muscle strength and bone density. Studies have shown that even ninety-year-olds have increased their strength by as much as two hundred percent in six weeks through weight training. I can imagine a vivid picture now—two old granddad's in the gym, with one lying down at the bench press beckoning to his friend, "Spot me, Clarence!"

The evidence overwhelmingly reveals that daily physical activity can slow the aging process and increase longevity by benefiting every part of your body. Exercising regularly can increase the number of immune cells moving throughout your body, which will help ward off infections. Weight training can prevent and even reverse bone density loss—and yes, osteoporosis is something men should be concerned about, too. Aerobic and stretching activities increase joint flexibility and help break vicious cycles of pain, stiffness, and inactivity that may lead to disability. Men who exercise regularly are also less likely to experience obesity, which next to smoking is the leading preventable cause of premature death. Additionally, those who are physically fit have healthier cholesterol and blood sugar levels.

As you age, your brain tissue gradually loses its density. Studies show that physical activity effectively helps to preserve tissue density in the brain, especially in the areas that affect daily functioning. Staying fit means being able to stay more focused and mentally capable of meeting the challenges of an active life. Regular exercise has also been found to be effective for managing stress, anger, anxiety, depression, as well as boosting self-esteem.

If you are over 50 and plan to start a strenuous exercise program, see your doctor first. If your doctor gives the thumbs up, ease into your routine by walking and stretching, then add abdominal and lower back strengthening exercises, followed by large-muscle activities such as weight lifting.

Establish Healthy Habits

> *"If you keep on doing what you've always done,*
> *you'll keep on getting what you've always gotten."*
> —Old Chinese Proverb

Your habits play a major role in how your future unfolds. Life never just happens. Instead it is a daily process of making choices and responding to every situation. If you are in the habit of continually making wise choices, then healthy consequences are likely to occur. It is a simple matter of sowing and reaping. By the law of the farmer you reap the harvest you plant. Successful men always have successful habits. *What you are ten years from now depends on what your habits are today.*

What is a habit? Simply stated, a habit is a behavior that you repeat so often that it becomes easy. The key to developing a habit is persistence. When you persist at developing any new behavior, it eventually becomes automatic. If you want more vibrant health, you must establish habits that produce it.

Men of significance don't accidentally drift to the top of the heap in life. They stay focused, disciplined, and committed each day to expend the energy to make things happen. Whether you are rich or poor, healthy or unhealthy, fulfilled or unfulfilled, you are experiencing a series of consequences based on your habitual thoughts and behaviors. Life always yields consequences, which you may like or dislike. You have the ability to turn the undesirable consequences of tomorrow into rewarding results simply by changing your habits today.

If you have an unhealthy habit—quit! If at first you don't succeed, quit again! And keep quitting the unhealthy habit until you do succeed, replacing it with good habits. (Nature abhors a vacuum, so take responsibility to create healthy habits to replace the unhealthy ones.) You are too smart to continue an unhealthy habit. Find something to use as a motivator to give you the strength to change your life, as I did with the humiliation I felt when the woman taunted me about my excess weight.

Create Financial Health and Well-Being

> *"Money is better than poverty,*
> *if only for financial reasons."*
> —Woody Allen

Robert Kiyosaki, author of *Rich Dad Poor Dad*, says, "The main reason people struggle financially is because they have spent years in school but learned nothing about money. People learn to work for money . . . but never learn to have money work for them." He explains that the key to financial freedom is a person's ability to convert earned income into passive income and/or portfolio income. If you are like many Americans, by the time Uncle Sam gets paid, you have managed to spend every remaining cent—at least! From a self-imposed position of weakness, you are not in a position to consider the concept of passive or portfolio income.

The secret is to "fatten your purse." In George Clason's book *The Richest Man in Babylon*, the wealthy Arkad asks a humble egg merchant, "If thou select one of thy baskets and put into it each morning ten eggs and take out from it each evening nine eggs, what will eventually happen?" The merchant said, "It will become in time overflowing, because each day I put in one more egg than I take out."

The first law of gold is, Clason says, *"Gold cometh gladly and in increasing quantity to any man who will put back not less than one-tenth of his earnings to create an estate for his future and that of his family."* The message is clear: to be financially healthy you must set aside a portion of your earnings for *you*.

Questions and Actions

1. Your number one recovery factor from stress is sleep. The adequate amount of sleep for the average person is 6-8 hours per night. Establish a routine of going to bed and rising around the same time each day.

2. Maintain a healthy diet. Eat light, eat often, and eat a variety of foods. For peak performance, eat higher amounts of protein during the morning and afternoon; and eat high complex carbohydrates, such as pastas and vegetables, during the evening. Make the front line of your diet grains, fresh vegetables and fruits, while staying away from high-fat, fried foods. Practice the 80/20 rule—80% of the time, eat a balanced diet, allowing a 20% margin for more lavish indulgence.

3. Exercise daily and try to make it fun and painless. A well-rounded exercise program should include activities that involve frequent moving, such as walking, jogging, biking, or swimming, three to four times per week. Perform light weight lifting and stretching exercises two to three times a week for strengthening bones, muscles, and connective tissue.

4. Use the following tips to start and stick with a health management program:

    *   Begin to think of yourself as a healthy person. As you think, so you become. The ancestor to every behavior is a thought.

    *   Write some attainable goals. Writing them down helps commit them to the sub-conscious and it gives you something to shoot for. If you don't have a destination in mind, how will you know when you get there?

- Set up rewards for your effort. Rewards will motivate you to keep moving toward your goals.

- Establish a social support network of friends who have an interest in healthy living.

- Place cues for reminders. For instance, if you want to drink more water each day, set a big bottle on your desk so you see it constantly. Put notes on your mirror or refrigerator door. A number of immensely successful men have claimed that they owe their success to writing reminder notes.

- Make exercise activities somewhat convenient. In other words, don't join a gym that is 50 miles away from your house, unless you happen to drive by there often. You can also set up exercise equipment in your home, such as a treadmill in front of the T.V. or hand weights in the bedroom that will enable you to exercise easily.

- Limit the amount of junk food that you keep at home, such as chips, candy, pastries, and others that are high in fat and refined sugar. Instead keep healthy food in store, such as fruit, nuts, and fresh vegetables like celery or carrots sticks.

- Practice good time management by budgeting. We each have 1440 minutes a day to spend. You can spend your time or burn it, but you can't bank what you don't use.

- Persevere until healthy habits are developed. Once an activity becomes a habit, it is easier to do it. Experts say that anything we repeat for 21 days becomes a habit.

- Profess your intentions to others and give them permission to offer valuable feedback. This will help you to maintain personal accountability for your actions.

5. Create financial success and well-being in your life by following three simple, yet profound principles:

- Live by the 80/20 rule. Set aside the first 10% of what you make as a tithe to give in gratitude back to the Universe through your church or a worthy charity. Set aside the second 10% as an investment in you and your family. Then learn to live on the other 80%.

- Stay out of debt. The grips of debt can be strangulating. Debt eats away at the heart of your financial resources. Tear up your credit cards and their exorbitant interest rates and learn to live on what you make in the present.

- Do what you love and the financial success will come. When you're in love with what you do, that love is contagious. It infects everyone around you in positive ways that will create opportunities beyond your wildest expectations.

Chapter 6

Commit to Being Mentally Tough

"He conquers who endures."
—Persius

In the twilight of his career Winston Churchill was asked to give a speech at the English prep school that he attended as a boy. The headmaster of the school assured the boys that this would be an historic moment in their lives. He lauded Sir Churchill as one of the great orators of the English language and urged the boys to write down every word he said because his speech was sure to be unforgettable.

When Churchill walked to the podium to deliver his speech, he gazed out over the top of his glasses and spoke the following words: *"Never! Never! Never! Never give up!"* Having said that, he walked back to his chair and sat down, his speech completed.

Though many of the students were disappointed by the abruptness of his speech, the headmaster knew that it may well have been one of his greatest, because it captured the essence of Churchill's character. His "never give up" attitude inspired an entire country to continue to fight under the bleakest of circumstances when others might have surrendered. Consequently, a great victory was won and the people of England experienced victory, in large part because of Winston Churchill's relentlessness.

Have you ever watched a stonecutter at work? He starts out with just a hammer to break open a giant boulder. He whacks the boulder as hard as he can and nothing happens. He whacks it again and again. Still nothing happens, not even a scratch or a chip. He continues to hit it again and again—maybe several hundred times or more without a scratch. If you were to observe him doing this you might ask, "Why does he keep engaging in this exercise of futility?" But the stonecutter is smart. He knows that it doesn't mean that you are not making progress, just because you don't see immediate results from your current actions,

He keeps hitting the boulder at different points over and over again, and at some point—perhaps on the five hundredth or one thousand and fortieth hit—the boulder splits cleanly in half, with no chips or broken pieces. Was it that single hit that caused the boulder to split open? Of course not. It was caused from the continuous pressure being applied in all the previous hits. If you consistently keep chiseling away, you too can break open any boulder that is blocking your path to success and significance. *Never give up!*

Maintain an Attitude of Gratitude

*"A grateful mind is a great mind
which eventually attracts to itself great things."*
—Plato

A group of humanitarian workers in Africa were perplexed by what they had observed with one of the tribes they were studying. This small tribe was poverty-stricken, although the other tribes in the same region were somewhat prosperous. The group spent years researching all aspects of the culture to try and understand this strange phenomenon. What made this tribe different than the others?

Their study revealed that this tribe had many similarities to the others: similar terrain, similar resources, similar customs and work habits. Only one small thing stood out that differentiated this small tribe from the rest: there existed no word in their tribal language with which to express gratitude. Could it be that through some quirk of evolution, they had forgotten how to say "thank you?" And could this loss of the spirit of gratitude have been responsible for their poverty?

By Plato's law, when you express gratefulness, you become great, and eventually attract great things. This group of researchers all but concluded that people become prosperous through maintaining a spirit of gratitude, and impoverished when they do not.

You may be thinking: "But you don't understand my situation. How can I be grateful in losing my mate . . . or in financial difficulties . . . or in failing health?" Please understand that gratitude is *not only* a reactionary emotion but also a causative energy. It is in the difficult times that you most need to "stir the pot" of gratitude in order to perpetuate and attract greatness into your life. You can choose to be weighted down by circumstances or lifted up by an optimistic spirit of thanksgiving. The grateful man draws to himself great things, while an ungrateful, complaining man often draws even more difficulty.

A teacher with the Peace Corps in Africa received a beautiful seashell from a man whom she had been assisting. Knowing that the ocean was some thirty miles away from where the man lived, and that there were no cars or means of motorized transportation in his remote village, she was a little confused. "Where did you find this?" she asked him. "Did a trader bring it to your village?"

"No, no," the man said, and then he told her that he had walked to a town on the coast.

She said, "You walked thirty miles to bring me a seashell? That is sixty miles round trip! Thank you!"

"Yes," the man acknowledged. "Long walk part of gift."

At times life may become difficult. Regardless of your circumstance, do what you can with what you have—right where you are. Focus on what you have rather than what you do not. You don't have to give thanks *for* the difficulties in life, but to attract greatness you must learn to give thanks *in* all things. And remember—*the long walk is often part of the gift!*

Go the Extra Mile

*"Diamonds are nothing more
than chunks of coal that stuck to their jobs."*
—Malcolm Forbes

Some time ago I was visiting with a man who happens to be in the same business as I. We shared our personal philosophies about customer service, and I mentioned that when I provide a service my goal is to exceed customer expectations. I want them to be more than satisfied with my work. He shrugged and said, "That's unrealistic! You can never 'more than satisfy' anyone. If we can simply meet their expectations, that's good enough for our organization."

I recently ran into that same man and asked how his business was doing. He winced and said, "Our business is sucking air these days. It has to be the economy." I replied that I was sorry to hear it, but was happy to report that my business was booming. I found it rather interesting that while we were in the same business, operating in the same economy, my business was doing well and his was doing poorly. Going the extra mile pays off.

You don't have to be a head and shoulders better than the competition to be successful. In fact, improving your performance by a small percentage will often place you ahead of the field. Take for example the Olympic runner who wins the gold medal while beating the second place opponent by a mere tenth of a second, or compare two professional baseball players, one carries a batting average of .275 while the other hits .300. The one who hits .300 only gets one more hit per forty times at bat than the other player, yet when it comes time for contract negotiation, he will often receive double the salary. Champions in both sports and business gain those small edges through a willingness to prepare a little harder, a little longer, and a little more frequently than others. *There is no elevator to success. You must take the stairs—one step at a time.*

... And Do Sweat the Small Stuff!

"A consistent man believes in destiny,
a capricious man believes in chance."
—Benjamin Disraeli

Most men would like to be the best at something, but few develop the discipline to do the little things to make it happen. In *Good to Great*, author Jim Collins describes the practice of "rinsing your cottage cheese," an analogy drawn from a disciplined world-class athlete named Dave Scott, who has won the Hawaii Ironman Triathlon six times. Scott's daily workout regimen consisted of riding his bike 75 miles, swimming 20,000 meters, and running 17 miles. And you thought your routine was grueling?

Scott did not have a weight problem, but he firmly believed that a low-fat, high-carbohydrate diet would give him an extra edge. So, even though he burned an average of 5,000 calories a day, Dave would literally rinse his cottage cheese to get the extra fat off. Now, there is absolutely no evidence that he needed to rinse his cottage cheese to win the Ironman, and that's not the point here. The point is that rinsing his cottage cheese was simply one more, small step, which he believed would make him a champion—one small step added to all the other small steps that contributed to a consistent regimen of super-discipline.

Imagine Dave Scott running the 26 miles of the marathon, in hundred-degree heat on the black, baked volcanic lava beds of the Kona, Hawaii coast after swimming a grueling 2.4 wave-tossed miles in the ocean and cycling 112 miles against ferocious crosswinds, thinking to himself, "Hey, compared to rinsing my cottage cheese every day, this isn't that bad."

Sweat the small stuff. Be dogged. Be determined. Be rigorous. Be diligent. Be focused. Be consistent. These are the things that will help you raise the bar of performance in your life. *Disciplined men maintain disciplined thoughts and habits, which produce world-class results.*

Perception Shapes Reality

> *"There is a point in every race when a*
> *rider encounters his real opponent*
> *and understands that it is himself."*
> —Lance Armstrong

A nationally known singer and songwriter, who is reputedly terrified of performing in front of a live audience, was once asked what she experiences before going on stage. She responded, "I get butterflies in my stomach. My palms begin to sweat. My heart begins to pound. And I feel like I'm going to have a nervous breakdown."

Another prominent entertainer who thrives on performing for live audiences was asked the same question about his experiences before taking the stage. He replied, "I get butterflies in my stomach. My palms begin to sweat. My heart begins to pound. And then I know I'm ready!"

Each of these performers experiences the same physiological responses going into similar situations, but each has a different perception of reality, based on their own emotional programming. Consequently, each has an internal dialogue about the experience. The first is telling herself a story about fear and anxiety, while the other tells himself that the increased emotional energy is serving to exhilarate his performance.

Your perceptions—what you imagine—shape your reality. You have a choice. You can let circumstances rule your life, or you can respond by moving through those circumstances, regardless of how unpleasant they appear, choosing to live with courage and purpose.

Men of significance possess a high degree of emotional and mental determination. They keep telling themselves a positive story, as they move undauntedly toward their goals. Many outstanding men who have been considered successful in their fields have faced major setbacks.

- **Abraham Lincoln** lost eight elections and failed twice in business.

- **Walt Disney**, who was dyslexic as a child, lost his first cartoon production company to bankruptcy.

- **Dr. Seuss**'s first book was rejected by 27 publishers.

- **John Grisham**'s first book was rejected by sixteen agents and 12 publishers.

- **Michael Jordan** was cut from his high school's varsity football team as a sophomore.

These are just a few examples of determined men who have overcome perceived failures and experienced great success. A writing professor at U.C.L.A. once reported that he received hundreds of rejection slips and pasted them on the wall of his office until they looked like solid wallpaper . . . before he sold his first story!

Each of these men kept telling themselves the story: "I think I can! I think I can!" What story do you tell yourself when faced with fear or adversity? Do you use that adrenaline driven energy to motivate you to perform at higher levels, or do you allow it to reduce you to a nervous wreck? You have the power to choose your response in any situation. Become aware of faulty perceptions, based on emotional programming from your past, which may cause defeating beliefs. Start changing those beliefs by using positive self-talk. Begin to tell yourself a different story.

It's not what happens to you that matters; it is what you do with what happens. *Your ability is not limited to your experience.* Don't sign a contract with the average, or negotiate an agreement with mediocrity, or pledge allegiance to the ordinary. You are capable of more than others expect of you, even beyond your most extravagant imagination.

Questions and Actions

1. Do you have a tendency to give up when the projects of life become too mundane, tedious, or difficult? Does success seem to continually elude you or stand just beyond your grasp? A few

men seem to be born with the strength to overcome any obstacle in their lives, but the majority of us have to work on developing our "stick-to-itiveness" muscles. Just like an athlete trains for competition by the gradual strengthening of his body, you can increase your mental and emotional stamina by training yourself to finish the races in your life. Start with small projects that you can finish in a day or two. Experience the taste of personal accomplishment and increase your levels of confidence by completing small goals. Success breeds success, and failure can breed even greater success, if you learn and grow from the experience. As your confidence grows you will find that you will create the capacity to pursue larger endeavors and challenges. Commit each day to move one step closer to your goals.

2. Perhaps you have become discouraged on your own journey towards your dreams. The walk has been longer than you expected; you are tired, afraid, and may have even taken a wrong turn or two. Don't give up. Trust the process. Each step you take will produce benefits and ultimately the long walk is worth the effort. It is part of the gift. If you continue to press onward in the direction of your dream, you will reap a far greater reward than the original object of your desire. You will experience a grander vision as you discover that, *instead of you building your dream, your dream has been building you.*

3. What can you do to go the extra mile today? Perhaps you could raise the bar of your performance by making five extra sales calls, or reading a journal article about a new development in your career field, or listening to a book on tape while you exercise at the gym, or learn three new words to expand your vocabulary. Ask yourself at the end of each day, "What did I learn and what did I accomplish today that moves me toward my goals?"

4. What are the levers in your life? What conjures up an all-consuming feeling of passion for you? Are you angry with someone or some thing? Perhaps you have an overwhelming

fear or phobia. Every one of these emotions will help to produce energy that can be utilized for leverage to strengthen you. The next time you experience fear or anger ask yourself, "How can I use the energy I feel at this moment to strengthen me for a positive outcome?"

5. Make a list of ten things in your life that need to be completed or finished and set out, one by one, to complete them. Every unfinished thing is an energy drain for you. And as you complete a project, you will create a greater space for new abundance to flow into your life.

Chapter 7

Commit to Living in the Present

*"Yesterday is history, tomorrow's a mystery,
today is a gift . . . that's why it is called the 'present.'"*
—Deepak Chopra

John Bunyan, the 17th century preacher and author of *Pilgrim's Progress*, once said that he was able to eliminate worry from two days of each week. He wrote: "There are two days in the week about which and upon which I never worry. Two carefree days, kept sacredly free from fear and apprehension. One of these days is yesterday and the other is tomorrow."

It won't do any good to pursue the past or to lose yourself in the future. The past no longer is, and the future has not yet come. Instead, fully focus on living in the present. You were created to carry the weight of twenty-four hours—no more. *Now* is the only time you can truly feel alive. Dwelling on the past or the future will only diminish your ability to experience true fulfillment in the present

Opportunities come your way each day and you must decide whether to take a chance or play it safe. Nothing is gained without the willingness to take some risks. It is that *Carpe Diem*—"seize the day"—spirit that beckons you to fully experience a life free of regrets and worry. This chapter may seem contradictory to the chapter that stresses the importance of goal setting, but it is not. Living in the present does not preclude planning for the future. In fact, the more you focus on getting the most out of the present, the better the future will be.

Let Go of Regret

> *"Forget regret, or life is yours to miss."*
> —Jonathan Larson

Perhaps you have heard the story of the man who owned an old hunting dog that fell gravely ill. He loaded up his lifeless companion and headed for the local veterinary clinic. Upon arrival the vet's assistant instructed him to carry his dog to the examining room and lay it down on the table. When the vet came in, she checked its vital signs and said, "Sir, I'm sorry to have to tell this, but your dog is dead."

"Why that's preposterous," the man demanded, "I want another opinion!" A Labrador retriever then entered the room, sniffed the dog from one end to the other, and nodded, "Uh-huh, this dog is dead."

The man refused to believe it. "I want another opinion!" he cried. Next, a cat came into the room, jumped up on the table and carefully inched her way up one side of the dog and down the other. She looked up and nodded in concurrence with the vet and the Labrador retriever, "This dog is dead."

The man still refused to believe it. He picked up his dog and stomped out, muttering something about another opinion. The vet's assistant handed him the bill on his way out the door. When he looked at his bill he couldn't believe it. "Three hundred dollars?" he shrieked, "Just to tell me that my dog is dead?"

She looked at him, shook her head apologetically and replied, "Sir, your bill would have been only fifty dollars, but we had to charge you for the *Lab report* and *cat scan*."

Like the man in this story, many of us carry around old dogs that need to be laid to rest. Those old dogs may be regrets from failed relationships, career choices, or other plans that didn't pan out. For whatever reason, we continue to carry those feelings or memories, toting them around like a smelly old carcass and deceiving ourselves into thinking they are still useful.

Regret is a thief that will rob you of health, happiness, and success, if you allow it. You may be experiencing the pain of regret right now; but face it, the chances of going back and reclaiming the past are no greater than stopping the sun from rising tomorrow morning. It just isn't going to happen!

How do you respond to failure or disappointment? Are there some old dogs that you need to lay to rest? Begin by turning around and looking in the right direction. Instead of bemoaning your past repeatedly saying, "If only . . . If only . . . If only," begin asking yourself smart questions such as, "What did I learn?" "What shall I do differently next time?" "How am I wiser because of this?" And affirm, "*Next time* I will make a better choice."

This is not an admonition to ignore the past. If you ignore the past you are destined to repeat it. Instead, glean the lessons you have learned and apply them to the present. Neither does this message imply that you should give up on a relationship or endeavor when the going gets tough. Instead make a deliberate, calculated decision to take the best course of action, without guilt or a sense of failure.

What direction are you facing? Do you find yourself dwelling on the past? Turn around; stop facing backwards and start taking ownership over the present. Live each day as if it were a life in itself and make the most of this moment—the only one you truly possess.

Clean Out Your Closets

> *"Simplicity, clarity, singleness:*
> *These are the attributes that give our lives*
> *power and vividness and joy."*
> —Richard Holloway, Anglican priest

Have you noticed that your life is often a reflection of the condition of your closets? The more cluttered your closets are, the messier your life seems to be. Many of us have stored things in our closets for years that we don't need or that no longer serve us. The same is true at an emotional level. We hold on to old emotional baggage that provides absolutely no benefit for our lives. In fact, it can become a hindrance to our growth and success.

Do you mindlessly store or stockpile old things, rather than actively deciding to either use them or lose them? To hoard is to operate from the fear of scarcity. Is the closet of your life so full of dusty clutter that somewhere deep under the piles of emotional junk you have misplaced your peace of mind? What gain is worldly success if the price is to lose your peace? Would success be worth that? Clean out your closets, sweep out all those tangled webs you've been weaving, and enjoy a life of simplicity.

Drop the Comparison

"And this I believe:
that the free, exploring mind of the individual human
is the most valuable thing in all the world."
—John Steinbeck

In *The Tassajara Bread Book*, Zen teacher Edward Espe Brown described a great truth that he learned from his kitchen practice. When Edward first started cooking, he couldn't get biscuits to come out the way they were supposed to. He would follow a recipe and try variations, but nothing worked. His biscuits just didn't measure up to the canned biscuits he had while growing up.

It didn't seem fair. Those biscuits of his youth were so easy to make. They came in an easy-to-open cardboard can. He just popped them open, put the pre-made biscuits on a pan, and baked them. They came out right every time. Now that's what biscuits were supposed to be, or so he thought.

Edward grew frustrated because, to his way of thinking, his biscuits never turned out right, even though the people who ate them would extol their virtues, eating one after another. In his mind, these perfectly good biscuits just weren't right, until one day Edward had an awakening, a real "a-hah" experience, about his biscuits.

"Not right, compared to what?" he asked himself. All this time he had been trying to make canned biscuits. Then came the revelation of tasting his biscuits without comparing them to some preconceived standard. They were wheaty, flaky, buttery, light, and earthy. They were exquisitely alive—in fact, they were much more satisfying than any memory of canned biscuits.

You may have spent years striving to look perfect, like a "canned biscuit" man, always calm, directed, energetic, and collected. Trying to produce a life with no dirty bowls, no messy feelings, or hindrances, can be a frustrating experience. A moment of liberation comes when you realize that your life may be fine just as it is. Only the insidious comparison to a neatly scripted, beautifully packaged product, made it seem insignificant or insufficient.

It may sound strange, but frequently a man with a poor self-image tends to be a perfectionist. If you feel inadequate or unsure of yourself, then you may start saying to yourself, "If only I achieve more or if only I try harder, then I'll feel better about myself and people will like me." Perfectionism, however, is never satisfied! Tragically, perfectionists think others will like them better for their perfection, but truthfully, it is just the opposite. People like to be around flexible, tolerant, and imperfect people like themselves. Go ahead and be what you were made to be, without being envious, full of pride, and comparing yourself with others, or trying to be something you are not.

Don't Just Do Something, Sit There!

"When I slow down,
I go faster."
—Old Japanese proverb

Perhaps you are old enough to remember those old Stan Laurel and Oliver Hardy comedy classics. One recurring scene portrayed an exasperated Oliver turning to his reticent little pal Stanley screaming, "Don't just sit there. Do something!" If you recall, each time Stanley reacted to Oliver's urgent demands by running around in a frenzy, accomplishing very little except to provide the audience with laughter from a comedy of errors.

There is a better way to be productive. Engaging in moments of stillness will enable your subconscious mind to function at deeper levels than usual, moving beyond the limits of self-imposed boundaries of logic, space, and time. You will experience moments of intuition, wisdom, creativity, and a heightened state of mental clarity. Everything you do is affected by your state of mind. If you speak and act with an unclear mind, chaos will follow you, as a shadow clings to its form. When you speak and act with mental clarity, peace and calm will be your faithful companions.

Let me clarify one thing: There is a huge difference between living *in* the moment and living *for* the moment. Living *for* the moment is focusing on the short-term, which often leads to binges, overindulgences, impulsive actions, or a variety of addictive behaviors. Living *for* the moment is like building your house on sand—it will wash away. *Shift happens!*

There is far more to life than just the few years we live on this planet. Don't indulge your ego at the expense of your soul. Living *in* the moment enables you to live from an eternal perspective by anchoring yourself in the present with an attitude of gratitude and appreciation for life, as well as a sense of accountability for the legacy you will leave for others.

As I stated earlier this chapter may seem somewhat paradoxical to some of the previous chapters in this book, but it is not. You can be a man of action who is disciplined and passionate about what you do, yet be totally calm and at peace in the present moment. Athletes refer to this state as being "in the zone." This is a state where you will achieve optimal performance as energy seems to flow easily and effortlessly.

Questions and Actions

1. What direction are you facing? Do you find yourself dwelling on the past? Turn around, stop facing backwards and determine to keep your focus on the present. You may have regrets from the past. We all do, but instead of saying "If only . . . ," when those thoughts of the past come up, say "Next time . . . ." With the dawning of each new day, commit to do your best, no more and no less. Also, keep in mind that your best may change from moment to moment. Don't beat yourself up when you fall down. Simply get up, determined to do your best next time.

2. Set aside some time to *thoughtfully* sort through and clean out your closets. Give away clothes and other things that you haven't used in years. By doing so you will create a space for greater abundance to flow into your life. As you clean out your closets, clinch the symbolism of this act. Begin to mentally go through the closets of your mind and do some cleaning and therapeutic purging there as well. Somewhere underneath the clutter lies the inner peace and contentment that may have been misplaced in your life.

3. Are you trying to be a "canned biscuit" man? Always trying to fit yourself or others into a neatly packaged plan? Standards are fine. We all need them to ensure continuity and quality in our lives, but we also need a sense of individuality without constantly comparing ourselves to others. Give yourself the freedom to be unique and march to the beat of your own drum.

4. Here is a simple exercise for relaxing and clearing your mind:

   Sit or lie down in a comfortable position. Open your mouth slightly and let your tongue rest gently against the soft palate between the roof of your mouth and the back of your upper teeth. Slowly inhale, expanding the diaphragm and abdominal area fully. Pause for a short moment. Exhale slowly, contracting the diaphragm and abdomen. Your exhale should take twice as long as your inhale. Pause between each breath. Close your eyes and let your breath flow back and forth from both your nose and mouth. Do not try to resist any thoughts that arise. Simply allow them to flow in and out of your mind, bringing your attention back to your breath. After performing this pattern for a brief time of five to ten minutes(or more), you will notice your mind and body entering a more relaxed and centered state.

   Meditations such as this can be very effective for both health and focus when they are 20 to 30 minutes long. You could begin doing this exercise for 5 or 10 minutes, and if so inclined, increase the time to more. If you happen to fall asleep that is

*okay. Your body will respond with what you need the most—
sleep or just a nice relaxed mind—which may create an opening
for a new idea, a solution to a problem—something of a
surprise to just POP into your consciousness. Or time to just
bask in gratitude. Slowing down your mind is often a real
learned skill in our sensory-overloaded culture. I know because
I sometimes feel like there is a racket ball game going on in my
head!*

Chapter 8

Commit to Becoming a Lifelong Learner

"By wisdom a house is built . . . through knowledge
its rooms are filled with rare and beautiful treasures."
—Solomon (Proverbs 24:3-4)

Knowledge is a key factor to long-term success and significance, *and* you don't have to possess a college degree to be knowledgeable. In fact, some of the smartest men I know do not possess college degrees. Instead they have taken the initiative to become self-educated. This type of education helps to deepen your understanding of what you believe and value. With self-education, unlike formal education that is geared mostly to build your resume, you design the curriculum. You become both teacher and student. The whole world becomes your classroom.

I met recently with a man who was despondent over losing his job because of corporate downsizing. He bemoaned, "I don't know what I'm going to do. This is all I know." I asked, "How long did you work at this job?' He replied, "Twenty-five years." Twenty-five years and that's all he knew how to do? I thought to myself, this guy could have learned to be a master craftsman at anything he wanted in twenty-five years, simply by spending 20-30 minutes a day working toward it. In that short amount of time each day, for 25 years not counting weekends, he could have invested nearly 4000 hours toward learning a new skill.

Don't allow that to happen in your life. Be a continual learner. Spend time each day sharpening your mental saw. Abraham Lincoln once said, "If I had eight hours to cut trees, I would spend six hours sharpening my saw." Your success is dependent upon your mental acuity. Become self-educated. Read books to exercise your brain muscle. If you don't have the time to become a bookworm, *become a tapeworm!* Check out books on tape at your local library and listen to them on your way to and from work each day.

Crossword puzzles are another great way to sharpen your brain power and expand your vocabulary. I work a crossword puzzle each day and recommend my coaching clients do the same. Studies overwhelmingly prove a positive correlation between how well you use the language and how successful you will be in career pursuits.

Collect advisors, mentors, consultants, coaches, and heroes in your field of interest. You will have to take the initiative to find them. They won't seek you. The more you talk to and absorb information from others who have succeeded, the quicker you will succeed. Open yourself up to help from all directions. Get interested. Get excited. Take up learning as a hobby. *If you stop learning today, you'll stop growing tomorrow.*

Be Teachable

*"It's what you learn
after you know it all that counts."*
—Coach John Wooden

The story is told about a college professor some years ago when the Eastern practice of Transcendental Meditation was popular. The man diligently studied this practice. One of his greatest aspirations was to go to India and sit in the presence of a great teacher who could impart profound knowledge to him. The day finally came when his aspiration became reality. During his first encounter with this great teacher, the professor was bubbling over with excitement, anxious to share all that he had learned. He talked tirelessly as the teacher listened. The guru offered him a cup of tea. The man nodded and kept talking as the teacher poured until the cup was overflowing. The man finally touched the teacher's arm and gently informed him, "Master, the cup is full, it won't hold any more." The teacher responded, "Yes, my son, and *you* are like the cup."

Perhaps the greatest obstacle to learning is not our ignorance but the knowledge we have previously attained. When we become full of our own stuff, it is difficult to receive or take in anything else.

In his book *Mastery*, George Leonard related a story that happened to him on a weekend retreat at the Esalen Institute outside of San Francisco. He had happened upon a mountain man, with the long black hair, bold moustache and rough-hewn clothing of a nineteenth-century outlaw, who was apparently giving an informal lesson on playing conga drums. The man was encircled by a group of about eight people. Leonard pulled up to one unoccupied drum and began to join the others, following the instructions as well as he could.

When the session ended, Leonard started to walk away, but the mountain man came after him, grasped his shoulder, and said, "Man, you *are* a learner. I want you to tell me how I can be a learner."

Leonard stood there speechless. This mountain man, an artist and sculptor who lived in the rugged hills of the Los Padres National Wilderness Area along the Big Sur coast of California, wanted Leonard to come to his place and look at his work, and tell him how *he* could be a learner, too.

Somewhat reluctantly, Leonard agreed to make the arduous journey to Los Padres to inspect the man's sculptures. When they arrived, the man showed some of his unfinished work and related to Leonard how he had lost his creative spark. He repeated his question again. "Tell me. How can I be a learner?"

Leonard gazed into the man's eyes for some time and replied, *"To be a learner, you've got to be willing to look like a fool."*

In order to yield to life's teaching, you must have the courage and the willingness to look like a fool. In the early stages of any significant new learning, you must surrender your hard-earned proficiency and risk looking foolish in order to rise to higher levels of proficiency. If you constantly try to stand on your own dignity, you will become rigid and unteachable. Always maintain a "beginner's mind."

Become an Agent of Change

> *"The significant problems we face*
> *cannot be solved at the same level of thinking*
> *we were at when we created them."*
> —Albert Einstein

One of the reasons that learning is so important is that it prepares you to deal positively and productively with change. When it comes to change, you have two choices: *you can choose to be a victim of change or you can choose to be an agent of change*.

Some sports enthusiasts think that Wayne Gretsky is the greatest hockey player to have ever played the game. In fact, they have dubbed him "the Great Gretsky." When people refer to you as the "great" anything, it indicates you are pretty good. Right? Yet if you notice, Gretsky is not any bigger, stronger, or faster than the other players on the ice. Someone once asked him what the secret to his success was. He replied, "I think many players skate to where the puck is, but I always skate to where it is going to be."

Continuous learning will enable you to skate to where the puck is going to be in your life. As Einstein said, you are not going to be able to solve today's problems at the same level of thinking that got you here. You must keep taking your mental game to a new level.

If you study business organizations, you know that any organization worth its salt will grow an average of ten percent per year or more. In the world of business there is no such thing as sitting still—companies either progress or regress. Life is dynamic, not static. *Shifts happen!* Your life is not any different than the life of a business. In fact, you are the C.E.O. of a corporation of one— *You, Inc.* You had better be doing something to help your personal business grow. If you are not moving forward, you are going to lose ground—no one stays the same.

Another important reason to keep learning and exercising your brain muscles is to stave off the effects of the aging process.

Senility is no longer considered to be an inevitable condition of aging. Most gerontologists today subscribe to the "use it or lose it" theory when it comes to mental alertness. I have seen too many men let their minds and bodies grow fallow as they approach their sixties. I don't want that to happen to me, and it doesn't have to happen to you. I know men in their late eighties who are vital, energetic, and productive. They didn't get that way by accident. They deliberately choose to do something each day to stay alert and vibrant.

Use or Lose Your Abilities

> *"Thinking is the hardest work we ever do,*
> *which is why so few of us ever do it."*
> —Henry Ford

Jesus told the parable of a rich man who was leaving on an extended trip. He called his servants together and delegated responsibilities. To one man he gave five thousand dollars, to another he gave two thousand, and to a third the rich man gave one thousand dollars. He gave to each according to their abilities.

Immediately the first man went to work and doubled his master's investment. The second did the same. But the man with the one thousand dollars dug a hole and buried his for safe keeping.

After a long absence the rich man returned and asked his servants to settle up. To each man who doubled his investment he said, "Congratulations for a job well done! From now on I want you to be my partner." The third man offered up several excuses. He was afraid that his master had such high standards and would demand the best allowing no room for error. And he was afraid he might disappoint his master so he secured a good hiding place to keep it safe and sound.

The rich man was furious. "That's a terrible way to live," he said. "It's criminal to live so cautiously!" The man was reprimanded for making no effort to at least produce a minimal interest on his master's investment. The rich man ordered him to give his thousand dollars to the man who risked the most, and then he was cast in prison for his "play-it-safe" attitude.

In this parable, the money represents natural abilities our Creator gives us, as well as skills we develop on our own. It is up to each of us to use our natural abilities *and* to develop new skills in the process. If you are faithful in doing so, there will be rewards. If you choose to let fear or lack of desire keep you from using your abilities, you not only lose them, but also become imprisoned by the fear that holds you back. Playing it safe poses the greatest risk.

Another message from the parable above is that you are accountable only for what *you* have been given, and not for what others have. The man who was given two thousand dollars and doubled it was regarded as highly as the man who started out with five thousand and doubled his. We are not all given the same abilities, but we are expected to know what we are given and to find ways to invest ourselves wisely.

Fail Forward

> *"Success is the result of good judgment.*
> *Good judgment is the result of experience, and*
> *experience is often the result of bad judgment!"*
> —Anthony Robbins

Thomas J. Watson, the founder of IBM, once reportedly summoned to his office a young salesman who had recently lost a substantial amount of the company's money in a bungled business transaction. After visiting for sometime about what the man had learned from the ordeal, Watson dismissed him to return to work. The young employee was a little surprised. "You're not going to fire me?" he asked. Mr. Watson shook his head and told the young salesman that he had just invested a large sum of money toward his education. Now the thing to do was to go out and do something with what he learned.

The question isn't whether or not you are going to fail, but how you are going to deal with it when you do. Will you fail forward or fail backward? Listed below are seven abilities of achievers that enable them to fail and keep moving according to John C. Maxwell in his book *Failing Forward: Turning Mistakes into Stepping Stones for Success:*

1. **Achievers Reject Dejection**—Those who base their self-worth on their performance often feel dejected and give up when faced with failure. Achievers keep trying because they have an internally based self-image. Rather than say, "I am a failure," they say, "I made a mistake." They keep the right perspective, take responsibility for their actions, but don't internalize failure.

2. **Achievers See Failure As Temporary**—Those who personalize failure see a problem as monumental, rather than momentary, while achievers view their predicament as temporary. Men hopelessly quit trying or believing in their potential for success when they view failure as being permanent.

3. **Achievers See Failures As Isolated Incidents**—They refuse to take failure personally. When they do fail, achievers see it as a momentary setback, not a lifelong catastrophe. A single incident will not tarnish their self-image.

4. **Achievers Keep Expectations Realistic**—The greater the accomplishment one pursues, the greater the preparation required to overcome obstacles and keep at it over the long haul. It takes time, effort, and the ability to overcome setbacks. Achievers don't get their feelings hurt when everything doesn't turn out perfectly.

5. **Achievers Focus on Strengths**—They maximize strengths and minimize weaknesses. Achievers keep their attention focused on what they can do, not on what they can't do.

6. **Achievers Vary Approaches to Achievement**—They keep trying and changing until they find something that works for them. Achievers are willing to vary their approaches to problems regardless of the comments or criticism of others.

7. **Achievers Bounce Back**—They have the ability to bounce back after making a mistake. Achievers see life simply as a

series of outcomes. Some are what they want, some are not. They learn from each and bounce back. Failure doesn't have to be final.

When you're playing to win, you fail forward regardless of what happens and don't take mistakes personally. An event that happened on baseball's opening day in 1954 illustrates the point. The Cincinnati Reds were playing the Milwaukee Braves. Each team fielded a young rookie who was making his major-league debut during the game. The Reds' rookie got hot at the bat and hit four doubles that day to lead his team to a 9-8 victory. The rookie for the Braves had a terrible performance going 0 for 5 at the plate.

The Cincinnati player's name was Greengrass, a name you may not recognize. The name of the Atlanta player, the one who didn't get a hit that day, was Aaron. You've probably heard of him. No doubt he was disappointed, but he didn't think of himself as a failure. He had worked too hard for too long and he wasn't about to give up that easily. And Hank Aaron went on to become the best home-run hitter in the history of baseball!

Questions and Actions

1. Learning practically any new skill will require you to look foolish. At times it will become necessary for you to give up some hard-earned competency in order to rise to the next level. If you're a better-than-average golfer and want to be an excellent golfer, you might well have to give up playing better-than-average golf as you take your game apart and put it back together again. This will be true for almost any skill, especially when you're stuck at a familiar and comfortable level. Don't allow yourself to stay in that "velvet rut." Be a sponge for learning. Soak up what others have to give. Each person is an expert of his own experience. Ask questions. Be inquisitive. And take advantage of every learning opportunity.

2. When you're not learning, you're not growing. *Do a check-up from the neck-up.* Continually look at your life to assess what's working and what is not. For those things that are not working,

change your strategy until you achieve what you want. Don't keep doing the same thing and expecting different results. That is called insanity.

3. Commit to learn something new and make improvements each day. Set aside at least ten minutes a day to read a book. Read all kinds of books, fiction as well as non-fiction. If you read ten minutes a day, you will complete on the average of one book per month—twelve books a year worth of new information. If you are absolutely too busy to read, buy books on tape and listen to them in your car on the way back and forth to work. The Internet is also a good resource that contains a wealth of knowledge on practically any subject right at your fingertips.

4. What are your natural abilities? Are you investing your time in them and developing other skills in the process? Sit down and make an inventory of your special talents. You may want to engage your mate or a close friend who may give you additional insight. Perhaps you have the ability for speaking, or teaching, or writing, or singing, or playing a musical instrument, or working with your hands as a technician, a mechanic, a carpenter, or a sculptor. Whatever your abilities may be, make a commitment to use them and develop others as well. Take some classes at your local community college. Enroll in a seminar. Attend a conference. Listen and ask questions. Travel to new places. Watch informative programs on television. Become a self-educated man.

5. How do you respond to failure? The question is not whether or not you are going to fail, but how you are going to deal with it when you do. Will you fail forward or backward? Don't let it get you down—*your past does not equal your future*. Simply learn from your mistakes, make adjustments, and try again until you succeed. Success is often found on the far side of failure.

Chapter 9

Commit to Having Fun

> *"Angels can fly only because*
> *they take themselves lightly."*
> —G. K. Chesterton

Two prime ministers sat in a room discussing affairs of state. Suddenly a man burst in, enraged with anger, shouting and stomping and banging his fist on the desk. The resident prime minister admonished him: "Peter," he said, "kindly remember House Rule Number Six," whereupon Peter was instantly restored to complete calm, then apologized, and withdrew from the room.

The politicians returned to their conversation, only to be interrupted again twenty minutes later by a hysterical woman waving her arms wildly and her hair flying about. Again the intruder was greeted with the words: "Marie, please remember House Rule Number Six." Complete calm descended once more, and she too withdrew with a bow and an apology.

When the scene was repeated for a third time, the visiting prime minister addressed his colleague, "My dear friend, I've seen many things in my life, but never anything as remarkable as this. Would you be willing to share with me the secret of House Rule Number Six?"

"Very simple," replied the resident prime minister. "House Rule Number Six is 'Don't take yourself so g--damned seriously!'" "Ah," said his visitor, "that is a fine rule." After a moment pondering, he inquired, "And what, may I ask, are the other rules?"

"There aren't any," replied his friend.

The message of this story is to *lighten up*. Fun and laughter are great medicine. They can help us get over our inevitable blunders, brain-farts, and communication foibles. Stop demanding to be taken so seriously. *Life is much too serious to take yourself so seriously!*

Ironically, having fun is one of the most important qualities of high performance living. Research indicates there is a direct correlation between fun and individual productivity. If you want to ensure personal success, make fun an integral part of your daily regimen.

Sadly, some men don't know how to have fun. They believe that having fun is a waste of time or unproductive. That is unequivocally untrue. Humor consultant and author C. W. Metcalf once wrote: *"Humor is a vital, critical element for human survival, and we often forget about it, and set it aside. We are told that laughter, fun, and play are un-adult, unintelligent, and unprofessional. Nothing could be further from the truth. One of the first indicators of the onset of most mental illness is a loss of a sense of joy in being alive."*

Consider how often you laugh on a typical day. Laugh experts tell us that prepubescent children laugh on the average of 110 times per day. As the years pass, the laughter quotient begins to drop drastically, and by the mid-forty's, adults typically laugh an average of less than eleven times per day. Where did our smiles go between childhood and adulthood?

Having fun plainly creates a healthier living environment. When you have a good laugh there is a release of the brain chemical endorphin that causes you to relax. At the same time there is a release of another brain chemical called norepinephrine which causes you to be alert. Muscle tension goes down and you end up calm and relaxed, yet energized and in a more creative, productive state. In the face of stress, laughter is the equivalent to emotional jogging. It helps your body to release tension and speed up the recovery process.

Jump Start Your Creativity

*"Joy is but the sign that creative emotion
is fulfilling its purpose."*
—Charles Du Bos

Creativity and fun walk hand in hand according to a study conducted by a team of psychologists at the University of Maryland. Researchers selected two groups of college students who were shown two different videos, then given a range of creative problems to solve. The first group viewed a five-minute film clip of comical bloopers lifted from various sitcoms and weekly television shows. The second group of students watched a math video that was very dry and technical.

As expected, the students in the first group, who had been laughing before the test, fared better at creative problem solving than the group who watched the math video. But what astonished researchers the most was the fact that the members of the first group proved to be *300 to 500 percent* more efficient at problem solving than their counterparts.

In other words, you can stimulate your creative juices and increase your performance by up to *five times*, simply by laughing and having fun before attempting to tackle problems. Where there is fun, there is enthusiasm. Where there is enthusiasm, there is energy. And in the presence of energy, creativity abounds.

Understand that all laughter is not the same when it comes to creativity. Laughing *with* someone is much different than laughing *at* someone. The first is a tool for enhancing creativity, while the second produces the opposite effect. Laughing with others should be nourishing, supportive, and confidence building as it brings people closer together in a spirit of collaboration.

Unstring Your Bow

"Nobody ever died of laughter."
—Max Beerbohm

The Greek historian Herodotus recorded a brief, yet telling story about King Amasis, who ruled in the 26th dynasty of Egypt from 570 to 526 B.C. Amasis had a daily routine of working diligently from dawn until noon, at which time he would abruptly quit whatever meetings or court proceedings were going on, and retire for an afternoon of leisure. He and his companions told stories, played games, traded witticisms, and indulged in the "free-flowing barley ale." Royal decorum wasn't a high priority in the afternoon activities of Amasis and his beer-drinking friends.

One day the advisors to the king reported to him that some people looked unfavorably at his afternoon routine. They thought a king ought to act in a more dignified manner—one that befitted someone of royal stature. The king listened attentively as the advisors pleaded their case, and then responded, *"When an archer goes into battle, he strings his bow until it is taut. When the shooting is over he unstrings it again. If he didn't unstring it, the bow would lose its snap and would be no good to him when he needed it in battle."*

Herodotus said very little else about the king, except that Amasis was the most prosperous leader in the history of Egypt. Do you get the message? You can't afford *not* to unstring your bow. Rest and relaxation are key ingredients for success and prosperity. Too much work, with too little play, can be detrimental to your health *and* your wallet!

Do you unstring your bow on a regular basis? If you were arrested for being good to yourself, would there be enough evidence to convict you? Create time in your schedule to relax. Go to a movie. Read a novel. Slip away for a fishing trip, a round of golf with some friends, or a weekend interlude with your mate, family, or friends. As you build a balance of leisure and relaxation into your life, you'll notice a livelier spring in your step and more snap in your bow.

Questions and Actions

1. Who said we have to be serious to be productive, efficient, or creative? You can have fun and get much accomplished at the same time. In fact, when you are having fun, you are the most engaged and focused. The more fun you have, the more you are locked into the present moment. The regrets of yesterday and anxieties about tomorrow fade away. Set aside regular time in your schedule to play and re-create. Go to the park and play with your children. Play with your adults friends. Make a date with your mate to go dancing, to a movie or concert, or to simply spend a quiet evening at home in front of a cozy fire.

2. Having fun doesn't have to be elaborate or expensive to have a positive impact. Following is a twelve-step program for fun developed by Dave Hemsath and Leslie Yerkes in their book *301 Ways to Have Fun at Work*. They playfully recommend that you read this list daily, poke fun at yourself frequently, and perhaps commit to putting one step a month into action for an entire year.

1) **Start with Yourself**—Don't wait on others to start the fun— become a *fun catalyst*. Evaluate how you spend your time and decide how you can liven up the spontaneous, fun spirit within yourself and others.

2) **Inspire Fun in Others**—Be a role model for fun. Take risks and don't be afraid to look silly. Give gifts to others that stimulate fun and spontaneity.

3) **Create an Environment that Encourages Fun**—Choose colors that enliven the environment, use music to brighten the mood, and funny conversation pieces. Surprise others by frequently changing things around.

4) **Celebrate the Benefits of Fun**—Champion the cause of having fun and its benefits. Be open to others' ideas about

creating an environment that everyone enjoys. Use fun as an excuse to spontaneously celebrate.

5) **Eliminate Boundaries and Obstacles that Inhibit Fun**—Fun is contagious. Once you remove the boundaries, it will travel fast bringing life and energy into everyone around you. Don't be afraid to confront people who discourage fun.

6) **Look for the Humor in Your Situation**—People usually want to be around someone who is fun and optimistic, rather than one who is gloomy and pessimistic. Be the man who can find humor in every situation and always be ready to laugh, especially at yourself—remember House Rule Number Six.

7) **Follow Your Intuition**—Be Spontaneous—There is no "appropriate" time or place for humor. Don't wait for fun to find you—make it happen when you or others need a boost. The elements of surprise will be refreshing and energizing.

8) **Don't Postpone Your Fun**—Fun should not be a reward for completing an assignment. Rather, it is the lubricant for performing well and working effectively with others. Don't put it off; make fun a part of your daily routine

9) **Make Fun Inclusive**—Fun should be shared by everyone—the more the merrier. When you exclude others, or direct it at them, it ceases to be fun. In fact, humor disguised as sarcasm can be hurtful.

10) **Smile and Laugh a Lot**—Smiling and laughing cost absolutely nothing. They require neither skills nor time to accomplish. Yet they have the most positively contagious impact on all your relationships. Greet everyone with a smile and laugh at yourself—others will join you.

11) **Become Known as "Fun Loving"**—One of the greatest compliments you can receive is to be known as a man with a

great sense of humor. Make it your personal mission to be the most fun-loving person you know.

12) **Put Fun into Action**—You will be remembered more for what you did than what you said. Grab a fun idea and take action. Have fun everyday. Borrow ideas from others or create your own, but most importantly—do it!

Chapter 10

Commit to Being a Difference-Maker

"Do all the good you can, by all the means you can,
in all the ways you can, in all the places you can,
at all the times you can, to all the people you can,
as long as you ever can."
—John Wesley

In the mid 1800s, Alfred Nobel was one of the world's top manufacturers of explosives and other materials used for destruction. He invented dynamite in 1866. The story is told that when his brother Ludwig died, Alfred picked up a copy of the local newspaper to read what it had to say about his brother. Instead he was shocked to discover that a dreadful mistake had been made. The newspaper had confused Alfred with his brother, and to his dismay, the obituary he was reading was his own.

The editors of the newspaper headlined his obituary with "The Master of Destruction Dies," as they wrote about Alfred's involvement with the invention of dynamite and elaborated on the powerful force of death and destruction he had brought into the world.

Alfred was devastated by what he read about himself in the newspaper. He wanted to be known as a man of *peace*, not destruction. He came to the realization that if his obituary was to be rewritten, he must do it himself by changing the course of his life. Alfred Nobel did just that! His financial contributions led to the creation of the Nobel Foundation, which awards prizes recognizing the world's great contributors in the fields of Physics, Chemistry, Medicine, Literature, and Economics. Most importantly, because of the Nobel Peace Prize, he is known throughout the world today as a man who embraced and perpetuated peace, rather than destruction.

Each of us has something to contribute to the world. We can choose to be a force for building up or tearing down. How will your obituary read? What will people say about your life? Like Alfred Nobel, you can write the script for the story of your life. In fact, you're writing it right now.

Champion a Cause Bigger Than You

> *"If you don't stand for something,*
> *you'll fall for anything."*
> —Unknown

As a young man in the early 1940s, Nelson Mandela was doggedly determined to make a difference in the freedom struggle of people in South Africa. He became politically active and was elected in 1942 to the African National Conference (ANC) where he impressed his peers with disciplined work and consistent effort in battling racism.

Mandela opened the first black legal firm in his country in 1952. During the entire decade of the 1950s, he was the target of various forms of repression. He was banned from practicing law, arrested, and imprisoned. He was forced to live apart from his family, moving from place to place to evade detection from government informers. He adopted numerous disguises, sometimes dressing as a common laborer, and other times as a chauffeur.

In 1962, Mandela was given a five-year jail sentence for inciting his countrymen to strike against apartheid and racial injustice. While serving his first sentence, he was brought up again on trumped-up charges and given life imprisonment. He spent nearly three decades in prison, most of the time in solitary confinement to keep him from influencing the other prisoners and guards. He was offered freedom several times under the condition that he denounce the activities of the ANC, but Mandela refused to abandon the principles for which he stood.

He finally gained release from prison in February 1990, at the age of 72. By that time, Nelson Mandela had become a worldwide symbol of the triumph of the human spirit over man's inhumanity to man. He won the Nobel Peace Prize in 1993 and accepted it on behalf of all South Africans who suffered and sacrificed to bring peace to their land. On May 10, 1994, he was inaugurated as the first democratically elected State President of South Africa and served in that office until June 1999.

A journalist once asked Mandela how he withstood the torture of almost three decades imprisoned in solitary confinement. His response was, "Oh, that wasn't torture; it was preparation. Those years prepared me to lead my country."

What causes are you championing? Is there something that you feel passionate enough about to risk everything for? Regardless of your age or the obstacles you face, if you have good *why* you can overcome any *what*. And when you become impassioned, others will follow. People will be drawn to you like a magnet. Courage will be echoed in your voice and hope will be reflected through your eyes.

Be a Catalyst for Positive Change

"You see things; and you say, 'Why?'
But I dream things that never were; and I say, 'Why not?'"
—George Bernard Shaw

It was a snowy desperate day at the Denver International Airport. Flight after flight had been canceled and lines at the airlines' service desks were snaking out of sight. Tension and tempers had been building by the hour, with customers sniping at the airline representatives—and at one another.

As I stood in line, feeling the pulse beat of the mob beginning to rise to frantic levels, I decided to try and change the mood—at least of those near me. So I announced, "I'm going to get some coffee. Anyone else want something to drink?"

I took down orders that echoed from a growing chorus of frustrated passengers, hustled off to the nearest coffee shop, and returned with a tray filled with drinks. That one act was enough to trigger a wave of good feelings and light heartedness among the group.

For that short moment, I emerged as the unofficial leader of this loosely knitted group of stranded travelers. Their attitude improved and their mood softened. The airline representatives even began to respond differently, without an air of defensiveness. I experienced firsthand the fluid role of a catalyst for positive change.

You can influence others through the sheer power of your own enthusiasm. You don't have to order people or direct them; simply inspire through your willingness to take action and to serve.

Stay Humble

> *"All streams flow to the ocean*
> *because it is lower than they are.*
> *Humility gives it its power."*
> —Lao Tzu

The measure of greatness in a man is the ability to subdue the ego to the point of needing no credit for accomplishments, to rise above the need for gratitude or applause, and to be independent of the good opinion of others. In other words, to do what you do simply because it is your purpose to do so. And there is no limit to the amount of good you can accomplish, if you are not concerned about who gets the credit for it.

Humility is about being focused and living purposefully, while remaining free of the need to be noticed. This is not about being a doormat, or being timid or weak. *Humble men don't think less of themselves, they think of themselves less.* There is strength in humility. The great teachers of the world have all possessed this gentle strength. They are ordinary men, yet extraordinarily powerful in simple ways. The ancient Chinese teacher and philosopher, Lao Tzu, referred to these men as peaceful warriors in the following poem:

Peaceful warriors have the patience to wait
until the mud settles and the waters are clear.
They remain unmoved until the time is right,
so the right action arises by itself.
They do not seek fulfillment, but wait with open arms
to welcome all things.
Ready to use all situations, wasting nothing,
they embody the Light.

Peaceful warriors have three great treasures:
simplicity, patience, and compassion.
Simple in actions and in thoughts,
they return to the source of Being.
Patient with both friends and enemies,
they live in harmony with the way things are.
Compassionate toward themselves,
they make peace with the world.

Some may call this teaching nonsense;
others may call it lofty and impractical.
But to those who have looked inside themselves,
this nonsense makes perfect sense.
And for those who put it into practice,
this loftiness has deep roots.

Embrace Diversity

"My religion is kindness and
my practice is tolerance."
—Mahatma Gandhi

If you look at coins minted in the U.S. you will see the Latin words *E Pluribus Unum* which mean "from many, one"—out of diversity comes unity. These words reflect a philosophy of inclusiveness, a simple and direct approach that enables us to experience a commonality of purpose with one another, and all human events. Our willingness to embrace diversity is one of the factors that have molded America into one of the greatest nations in the history of the world.

We are all unique in some way. In many ways our ideals may seem opposite from others we meet. But that seeming opposition may turn out to be complimentary ideals that add up to much more than the sum of their parts. They may compliment each other like night and day. The complimentary nature of opposites is apparent even in the field of science. Physicist Emilio Segre wrote, *"It is one of the special beauties of science that points of view which seem diametrically opposed turn out later, in a broader perspective, to be both right."*

One of the hallmarks of maturity is our willingness to accept another's sense of the truth without it invalidating our own, no matter how contradictory it appears. Regardless of our differences, we all belong to the family of mankind. The Native Americans from the Lakota Sioux tribe have an expression that describes this connectedness. It is *Mitakuye Oyasin*, which can be translated as "we're all related."

Do you ever feel disconnected from or at odds with others because of differences? Maybe their skin is a different color, or they have a different political persuasion, or perhaps they have a different religion than you. Make a commitment today to suspend judgment and simply practice tolerance for others who are different than you.

Give Credit Where Credit is Due

> *"I want to know God's thoughts . . . the rest are details."*
> —Albert Einstein

The story is told of a group of scientists who perfected the cloning process. They finally achieved the "unachievable"—creating a human being. The lead scientist, a rather arrogant type of fellow, smugly sat down and wrote God a letter informing him that, "we will no longer need your services." God received his letter and immediately came calling.

God asked, "What's up with this?" The man replied, "Yes, we have created the perfect human being. A human more perfect than even you can create, so we won't need your services anymore." He even had the audacity to challenge God to a man-making contest. God accepted the challenge.

They went outside and God said, "You go first." The man bent over and began scraping some earth together, but God quickly stopped him and declared, "Hold it—go get your own dirt!"

I believe that life is no accident and that nothing is formed by chance. Everything has its reason for being created. The available evidence of the biological sciences supports the proposition that the universe is specially designed with life and humankind as its fundamental goal and purpose. The more we learn about the cosmos, the better we understand how it is uniquely suited and custom-made with the exact specifications for our existence. *As you build your bridges to success, remember who owns the ground upon which you build.*

Questions & Actions

1. What do you want to be remembered for? What would you like people to say about you after you're gone? Sit down and write your own obituary. Better yet, write three obituaries about yourself. Write one from the perspective of what your family members have to say about you. Were you loving and kind? Did you validate those in your life who were closest to you? Was your presence in their life uplifting and encouraging? Next write an obituary from the perspective of a friend in your community. Were you helpful to those in need? Did you always have something positive to say when the chips were down for others? Were you involved in causes that promoted peace and harmony in your world? Write one more obituary from the perspective of a peer or co-worker. Did you work with integrity? Were you a promise-keeper? Were you a benevolent leader, or a faithful follower? Learn from this experience as you commit to write a happy ending for your life.

2. How will you leave the world a better place than when you arrived? Build your legacy by championing causes that make a difference in your world. What are some worthy causes that you can champion? Think globally, but act locally. Find ways to get involved in your community to make a difference.

3. Are you a catalyst for positive change? To become a catalyst you must first recognize the need for change and be willing to take some bold steps to remove the barriers. Don't be afraid to challenge the status quo to acknowledge the need to do things differently. Start thinking "out of the box." As you champion the change, enlist others in your pursuit and lead by example.

4. Practice random acts of kindness and humility. Give anonymously to people in need, without asking for or expecting recognition or praise in return. Look at each relationship—your family, your friends, even strangers you meet on the street—as an opportunity to give. Among the greatest gifts you will give are acceptance and tolerance of others who are different than you.

5. Of course there will be difficult times in life when, despite our best efforts, we sometimes end up facing insurmountable obstacles. When life's problems get bigger than you, to whom will you turn? *A Divine wind is always blowing, but it is up to you to raise your sails.*

Conclusion

The film *Lawrence of Arabia* depicted a powerful scene where Lawrence's army had undertaken a brutal ten-day death march through the desert. The soldiers were near death from dehydration when they spied an oasis and eagerly plunged into the water. When Lawrence took a head count of his men, he noticed that one of the camel boys was missing. They found the boy's riderless camel near the back of the camp and surmised that he had fallen off during a sandstorm.

"We must go back and find him," Lawrence shouted to his men. But they refused to venture back into the merciless inferno of sand.

"Master," they begged, "it is Allah's will that the boy did not return with us. His fate was written by God. We must not interfere."

Lawrence angrily mounted his camel and headed back into the desert. His men stood there, shaking their heads in bewilderment. "Now we've lost him, too," they groaned, as they returned to the comfort of the oasis. Two days later an iridescent image emerged from the heat wave. "It's Lawrence!" the men shouted, "He has found the boy!" They ran eagerly to assist him. Lawrence leaned over and handed them the boy who was unconscious. He looked into their eyes and said in a raspy whisper, "Remember this: Nothing *is written* unless you write it."

Think about it. Nothing is written unless you write it. Your life right now is the result of the choices that *you* have made.

Here is a secret you may not want to hear: most men will not live a life of significance. There is a difference in knowing what to do and doing what you know. It takes courage and commitment to do what you know. John Hancock has the largest signature on the Declaration of Independence. In fact his name has become synonymous with the word *signature*. It is said that after he signed the Declaration, he turned to his colleagues and said, "I don't want the king to have any problem finding my name." Now that is courage and commitment with a capital C!

Why do what most men can or will, when you can do what most men can't or won't. It may not happen in a week, a month, or a year. But eventually you will split that boulder in half if you persist. You are a difference-maker!

You have the power to create a great destiny if you will commit to:

- *Know and be yourself*
- *Be a promise-keeper*
- *Get excited about something*
- *Build quality relationships*
- *Take care of your health*
- *Be mentally tough*
- *Live in the present*
- *Become a lifelong learner*
- *Have fun*
- *Be a difference-maker*

You may have noticed phrases, quotes, and anecdotes that bear close resemblance to those that appear elsewhere in my writing. This is not a matter of sloppy editing. I am purposely repeating myself. I keep reshuffling words in hope that one day I may say something that profoundly impacts your life and mine. Like you, I continue to wrestle with many of these issues that are not easily resolvable or easily dismissed. I run at them again and again because I am not finished with them and may never be. This is a work-in-progress about a life-in-progress. We're in this together. See you at the top!

Tom Massey